# The Essential Handbook for Musicians Who Teach

A practical guide for instrumental and singing teachers

Dr Kerry Boyle and Diane Widdison

With thanks to John Shortell, Dr Sarah Upjohn and Chris Walters for their expert knowledge and help.

© 2021 by Kerry Boyle and Diane Widdison
All rights administered worldwide by Faber Music Limited
First published in 2021 by Faber Music Ltd
Bloomsbury House
74–77 Great Russell Street
London WC1B 3DA
Cover design by Adam Hay Design
Page design and typesetting by Elizabeth Ogden
Printed in England by Caligraving Ltd
All rights reserved

ISBN10: 0-571-54210-7
EAN13: 978-0-571-54210-9

To buy Faber Music publications or to find out about the full range of titles available please contact your local retailer or Faber Music sales enquiries:

Faber Music Limited, Burnt Mill, Elizabeth Way, Harlow, CM20 2HX, England
Tel: +44 (0) 1279 82 89 82    Fax: +44 (0) 1279 82 89 83
fabermusic.com

# Contents

**Foreword**   7

**Preface**   9

**1 Who is the teaching musician?**   11
    Early teaching experiences
    Understanding teaching situations
    The professional portfolio musician

**2 Settings and workplaces**   17
    Instrumental and singing teaching in the UK
    Music services and music education hubs
    Private teaching
    One-to-one tuition in schools
    Online instrumental tuition
    Working in community music
    Things to remember in all teaching situations

**3 Getting business ready**   29
    The different types of employment status
    Who decides my employment status?
    What if my employment status seems wrong?
    Getting paid
    How to set your own rates
    Holiday pay
    Am I getting all my employment benefits?
    School teachers' pay and conditions (STPC) and zero-hour contracts
    Contracts
    Teaching for agencies and other organisations
    Self-promotion
    Finance
    Insurances
    The benefits of joining a trade union

**4 What is good teaching?**   45
    What is the main purpose of learning music?
    Planning for lessons
    Communication with parents and carers
    Taking on students from other teachers
    How structured should lessons be?
    Key lesson components
    The importance of warm-ups
    Developing aural skills
    How do instrumental and singing teachers teach?
    The development of metacognitive skills
    Age, learning development and motivation
    Teaching beginners
    Teaching intermediate learners
    Teaching advanced learners
    Group teaching
    Are exams a good idea and what are the alternatives?

**5 Keeping safe**   65
    Safeguarding
    Responsibility
    Abuse and its effects on child development
    Child abuse
    How to respond if a student confides in you
    Reporting child abuse and the child protection system
    Good practice for instrumental and singing teachers
    Allegations against teachers
    Disclosure and Barring Service (DBS)
    Safeguarding and child protection training

**6 Health and well-being for musicians**   81
   Musculoskeletal health
   Vocal health
   Mental health
   Performance anxiety
   Hearing issues
   Further support

**7 Equality, diversity and inclusion**   91
   Understanding discrimination
   Understanding diversity, equality and inclusion in music education
   Definitions of discrimination
   What would you do?
   Overcoming barriers to musical learning
   Technology-assisted learning
   Adapted instruments

**8 What next?**   100
   What is CPD?
   Where to start?
   Taking stock
   Planning your CPD
   Formal learning opportunities
   Accreditation and qualifications
   Reflective practice
   Sharing best practice
   Connecting to a community of practice
   Social learning activities and initiatives

# Foreword

It is important to make the distinction between 'music teachers' and 'musicians who teach'. The former almost always have teaching qualifications and primarily undertake classroom teaching. The latter are often highly skilled performers who may have no formal teaching qualifications. They can give one-to-one lessons or teach small groups; they may also direct ensembles such as trios and quartets or large choirs and orchestras. This book is a welcome tool for all such musicians who teach, helping to maximise their skills and organise their working lives.

Research has shown that learning an instrument and developing performing skills is very important to the development of children and young people. As well as enhancing hand-to-eye skills, it encourages teamwork and reveals the importance and satisfaction of working closely with others. Of course, it also gives young people a life-long love of music and the arts.

Teaching is a very important part of the portfolio careers of professional musicians. While they have a high level of knowledge about the practicalities of playing their instruments and working with other musicians, they need support in many other matters. These include advice on child protection and safeguarding; health, safety and well-being, and where to find opportunities for continuing professional development and career advancement.

This book fills an important gap in the literature in this area and is a vital guide and companion for all instrumental and vocal teachers.

**John F Smith OBE**

*John Smith began his career as Principal Tuba in the English National Opera orchestra before joining the Musicians' Union, where he was General Secretary from 2002–2017. He is President of the International Federation of Musicians (FIM) and Chairman of the Royal Society of Musicians and the collective management organisation, PPL. John was awarded an OBE for Services to Music in the Queen's Birthday Honours list in 2020.*

# Preface

Instrumental and singing teachers are central to the culture of music education, contributing both to the musical development of individual students and to the musical life of schools, colleges, universities and music centres. Teaching can be rich and rewarding work for musicians as it provides opportunities to share music and nurture future generations of instrumentalists and singers. In addition, teaching can be a valuable source of income as part of a portfolio career involving various other roles and individuals can enter this form of teaching from a range of musical backgrounds.

This is an informed, accessible guide to key aspects of work in this area that supports musicians in their teaching, whatever their background, interest or level of experience. It contains useful, practical information for those considering teaching whether as a first career or as an addition to their professional portfolio.

The book starts with a summary of the various teaching situations, the expectations and the significant aspects of the work in different environments. It explores a range of employment considerations for workers in this field, and various practical aspects of instrumental and singing teaching including planning, motivation, development, teaching techniques and lesson content. The remaining chapters offer advice and information on practical topics such as contracts, employment rights, safeguarding, health and well-being, inclusion and continuing professional development.

For the sake of clarity, *instrumental teacher* and *teacher* describe all instrumental and singing teachers.

# 1
# Who is the teaching musician?

Instrumental and singing teachers working in the UK are not required to complete any formal training course or qualification, unlike classroom music teaching, which requires a degree in music and a PGCE (Postgraduate Certificate of Education) or other teaching qualification. Musicians come to teaching through a variety of routes – some start while still studying, and others begin much later, perhaps having worked as performers or in other professions entirely. They come from a wide range of formal and non-formal musical backgrounds; they may be formally trained, taught through peer- or social-learning models such as the brass band approach, or they may be self-taught. The role of the teaching musician varies with each route, and will inform the way individuals develop their identity and approach as teachers.

Teaching musicians work with children and adults of all ages, either on a one-to-one basis or in groups, in a range of settings including schools, colleges, universities, conservatoires, homes or community-based facilities. Instrumental teachers typically work in a variety of locations with the freedom to combine various forms of employed and self-employed roles. For example, they may be a self-employed teacher in various settings, engaged by a local authority music service to teach in schools, and/or work as an employee in schools, colleges, universities and music centres.

Whilst it can take time to establish a good reputation as an instrumental or singing teacher and build a portfolio, this arrangement works well for musicians who perform regularly, offering flexibility and a valuable source of reliable income. In many cases, musicians promote themselves locally to build a teaching practice, although schools, universities, music services and other educational institutions also regularly advertise vacancies. Teaching can be combined with other roles in the music industry such as composing, performing, directing, examining, or with work in another sector entirely.

### Key features of instrumental and singing teaching in the UK
- Can take place in a variety of settings.
- There is no set curriculum.
- No formal training is required.
- There are no regulations.
- Provides high levels of professional autonomy.

*Professional autonomy*
In the UK, instrumental teaching is not currently subject to any formal regulation and there is no imposed or recognised curriculum. Those working for music services or in schools might expect to be observed by senior staff, but private instrumental or singing teachers are not subject to inspection or observation. Instrumental teachers therefore generally experience greater levels of professional autonomy than those working as classroom teachers in mainstream education. There is no official curriculum for instrumental teaching, but for many teachers the exam grade system provides a guide to progression, though you can choose to avoid this approach entirely.

*The apprenticeship model*
As an instrumental teacher, your role is central to the culture of music and music education, often providing the primary source of instrumental skills. A large amount of instrumental teaching is arranged on a one-to-one basis in what is often referred to as the *apprenticeship model*, through which students receive an 'apprenticeship' in instrumental playing and effectively learn how to be a musician. The teacher, as role model and mentor, develops the student's practical skills and provides an understanding of the world of instrumental music. As skilled musicians working in a variety of professional roles, teachers offer a realistic model of a future career for music students.

# Early teaching experiences

Many musicians begin teaching in an informal way with other students, friends or relatives, so it may not feel like real teaching at the time. The following examples represent common ways young musicians first experience the role of teacher.

*Peer support in schools*
Early teaching experiences are often in school, where students help their peers either on an informal basis or in a formal arrangement established by a teacher. In some cases, the student helps younger learners in return for additional or longer lessons on their chosen instrument.

*Teaching friends and family members*
This is a common way for students to begin one-to-one instrumental teaching. These early teaching arrangements are often encouraged by parents and family members. Lessons may involve payment but are sometimes provided free of charge.

*Student teaching*
Many students in higher education teach as a source of income, often with the support of teachers and music staff. This may involve other students as well as adults and children living in the local area. Opportunities can be advertised in music departments or between students and some instrumental teachers offer the chance for their students to teach.

> **Before starting out, consider the following:**
>
> - **Who?** What age and standard of students are you most comfortable teaching? Beginners? Advanced students?
> - **What?** Are you interested in group teaching and if so, what types of groups? Small? Large?
> - **Where?** In which setting will you work? Will you provide private studio tuition, peripatetic teaching or work in specific institutions?

## Understanding teaching situations

> **Terms used to identify instrumental and vocal teachers**
> - VMT (visiting music teacher)
> - Peripatetic music teacher ('Peri')
> - Private music teacher
> - Specialist instrumental teacher

As a freelance or peripatetic teacher, you can be engaged to provide tuition on your own instrument or a range of instruments, in one-to-one lessons, in small groups, large groups, or whole class and ensemble teaching situations. New instrumental and singing teachers therefore need to learn to adapt their existing skills and understanding to each teaching situation. You will need to consider specific practical aspects such as timetabling, and lesson arrangements such as room bookings and staff support when necessary.

If the school or college view you as a visiting musician with specialist knowledge, they may provide additional support, for example during large group lessons, and in some cases these can also provide a development opportunity for school teachers or support staff. In some schools, peripatetic teachers are welcomed as members of the music team and offered ensemble direction opportunities, but it is also common to be engaged simply as a visiting music teacher in the department.

All institutions will have specific expectations and teachers are required to respond accordingly. It is therefore important for you to have a secure sense of your role in each teaching environment, and to have a strong sense of what matters most in any teaching and learning situation. In developing your approach, you may be influenced by your own teachers and experiences in music education, especially if you are just starting out. The ability to adapt and share your knowledge with the next generation of students is what makes instrumental and singing teaching both creative and rewarding for musicians.

## The professional portfolio musician

When musicians are balancing multiple roles in portfolio careers, it is vital that there is minimal conflict. All forms of employment should be given the necessary time and personal and professional commitment. Consider, for example, the impact on students when a teacher cancels lessons at short notice because alternative professional work has become available. Take time to plan your diary on a weekly, monthly and annual basis to avoid conflict and maintain a high professional standard across all working commitments.

Successful portfolio musicians adapt their key understanding and skills to each professional situation, recognising the nature and expectations associated with each role. A solo performance on the concert stage requires different skills and behaviour to those required to lead a workshop or give a one-to-one lesson. It is therefore vitally important to recognise and refine your understanding of the various roles in which you are engaged.

> **Musical identities**
> 
> Consider the following roles. How may the musician's understanding and skills need to adapt for each? What forms of communication might be required? What are the professional characteristics of the role? What is the status of the individual in each professional setting?
> 
> | | |
> |---|---|
> | Private teacher | Orchestral performer |
> | Band member | Solo performer |
> | Conductor | Choral director |
> | Accompanist | Youth ensemble director |
> | Adjudicator | Examiner |

The portfolio career demands organisational and entrepreneurial skills and an ability to negotiate in various professional contexts. The following case studies are from portfolio musicians working in the UK. In each, the musician combines a variety of roles to suit their personal interests and goals.

*Case study 1*
Kimora is a violin teacher. She provides one-to-one violin lessons on a freelance basis in her own home, at a primary school and at a secondary school. She is also employed to teach on a one-to-one basis in an independent school. In addition, she is employed by a regional music service to provide individual violin lessons and direct string ensembles at a local music centre.

*Case study 2*
Belmin is a guitarist and guitar teacher. He provides one-to-one tuition on a freelance basis in his own home and at two secondary schools. In addition, he performs professionally with various bands and works as a session recording musician.

*Case study 3*
Debbie is a flautist, flute teacher and ensemble director. She works on a freelance basis, teaching in her own home and at a secondary school where she teaches individuals and directs a student ensemble. In addition, she is employed on an hourly basis to teach undergraduate and postgraduate students at a local university and performs professionally in various orchestras and ensembles and as a solo flautist. Debbie also manages and directs a local youth orchestra.

*Case study 4*
Paul is a trombone player, performer and conductor. He is employed on a part-time basis to deliver classroom music lessons, individual brass lessons and to direct a brass ensemble at an independent school. He has enjoyed a successful career as a professional performer and continues to perform regularly with various ensembles. Paul also works as a freelance conductor and is employed to direct a regional youth orchestra.

*Case study 5*
Simon is a freelance percussionist and teacher. He performs professionally with various orchestras and ensembles and is regularly employed on a sessional basis for gigs, shows and tours. He also works as a freelance tutor, teaching individual students in a secondary school.

It is widely acknowledged that the majority of musicians will be involved in some form of teaching during their career. Realistic career preparation should therefore involve the development of a teaching approach, including a range of skills that can be adapted and applied in various situations. The following chapters will provide valuable information, insights and tips to help make this experience rewarding and successful for all involved!

> **Top tips: how to develop a portfolio career as a musician**
> - Know your strengths and promote them.
> - Start with what you know and build from there.
> - Be prepared to try new roles.
> - Be prepared to be flexible and adaptive.
> - Be on the lookout for new opportunities.
> - Be prepared for every situation and do the best job you can in each context.
> - Prioritise communication and admin or it will take over!
> - Learn how to balance your time and don't overload yourself.
> - Remember that doing music every day is success, whatever the role – and enjoy it all!

**Further reading:**
Bennet, D. (2013), *Understanding the classical music profession: the past, the present and strategies for the future,* Farnham: Ashgate
Mills, J. (2007), *Instrumental teaching,* Oxford: OUP

# 2
# Settings and workplaces

This chapter introduces the educational settings in which you might work as a teaching musician, including schools, music services and music education hubs as well as community and outreach situations. We will explore the key considerations of teaching individuals, small groups, whole classes and ensembles as well as working with adults.

## Instrumental and singing teaching in the UK

Since the 1990s, instrumental teaching in the UK has seen a period of significant change with a growth in group and online tuition. Developments in technology have enabled access to a wider range of styles and cultures, and students now enjoy a greater range of ways to engage with the study of music. Students are increasingly interested in taking instrumental and singing lessons in a range of musical styles. As teachers we need to adapt, just as education institutions have by running higher education courses in diverse musical styles and disciplines including jazz, popular music, musical theatre, music technology, arts management and music education.

Developments in group and whole-class teaching (and changes in the goals of those involved in music education) mean that instrumental teachers need to be flexible and accommodate a range of interests and styles that may or may not reflect their own experience as musicians.

Before deciding what specific range of styles and instruments you might prefer to teach, it is important to understand the main features of the work in each context. The following sections provide an introduction to the role of the musician as teacher in a range of professional settings.

## Music services and music education hubs

### What is a music service?
Regional and Local Authority music services are a key employer and engager of instrumental and singing teachers in the UK, providing a range of activities in schools and music centres, including instrumental and vocal lessons, choirs,

bands, orchestras and ensemble activities. Instrumental teachers working for music services are part of a larger workforce of teaching staff with managerial structures and administrative support.

Music services are usually responsible for the generation, allocation and administration of teaching, including invoicing, though teachers can often generate new opportunities themselves through workshops and taster sessions in schools and music centres. Music services may also provide continuing professional development (CPD) opportunities for instrumental teachers and advice and training for schools.

*Rates of pay*
On a practical level, music services usually operate by charging schools and/or parents for the services of instrumental and singing teachers, but there is no standard model and so both fees and rates of pay can vary. With increased numbers of students having access to instrumental tuition in a wider range of styles and instruments, music services are required to adapt and remain competitive by providing a high standard of tuition at a competitive price.

*Working for a music service*
When working for an organisation of this kind, you are usually expected to deliver individual, small group, large group or whole-class tuition in schools. The work is mostly part-time and paid hourly, though full-time positions are sometimes available. Group tuition can be a challenging prospect if your only experience is one-to-one or ensemble-based, but this can be a rewarding opportunity if you take the time to plan and prepare for lessons. In most cases you can expect to receive support from both the music service and the school in which the sessions are being delivered. (For advice relating to lesson planning and preparation see **Chapter 4: What is good teaching?** page 45.)

You may be involved in extra-curricular activities including ensemble direction. These opportunities also represent valuable learning experiences for early-career teachers and can be a real highlight for many. Again, careful and creative repertoire selection and planning with consistent emphasis on the interests and abilities of ensemble members is the best way to ensure that all involved get the most from these activities.

*What is a hub?*
In England, music education hubs commonly involve a range of organisations including local authorities, music services, schools, community groups and arts organisations working together to deliver a joined-up music education provision, responding to local needs. Hubs are coordinated by the hub lead organisation

(often a music service), which takes responsibility for the funding and governance of all partnerships, activities and initiatives.

> **Teaching in music services and hubs**
> **Type of employment:** you are employed or engaged by the music service on a full- or part-time basis.
> **Role of the teacher:** your role is to deliver one-to-one, group and whole-class tuition and ensemble direction in schools and music centres.
> **Key skills:** you are required to have secure instrumental skills and an adaptable teaching approach across a range of settings. You need strong communication and organisational skills.

# Private teaching

Private teaching remains the most popular form of tuition for aspiring and advanced instrumental students. This model, represented in the conservatoire culture of advanced music making, is generally regarded as the most effective way of training successful instrumentalists and singers. For this reason, parents hoping to encourage musical interest in their children will often seek out private teachers rather than opting for group tuition in schools.

*Where can private tuition take place?*
The majority of teachers provide private lessons in either their own home or their students' homes. Private tuition is convenient and provides a degree of flexibility that is so important to many musicians as it can be carried out alongside freelance or part-time employed work in other locations. This form of tuition also takes place in schools, colleges, universities and conservatoires. Other venues include private rented studios, independent schools and music shops.

*Rates of pay*
The majority of private tuition is on a one-to-one basis, although group tuition can be more lucrative. Tuition fees vary depending on the region and the experience of the teacher. Each teacher can set their own fees and charge for lessons on an hourly or pro rata rate. As the teacher, you are able to specify terms including the nature and frequency of payment and the period of notice.

*Pros and cons of private teaching*
As a private instrumental teacher you have a greater level of professional autonomy than if employed by a music service or educational institution. As with any form

of freelance work, there are risks for private teachers — students can simply find another teacher or choose an alternative instrument if they are not satisfied. However, there are also significant benefits as you have the ability to increase or reduce your working hours to suit professional or domestic commitments.

*What is involved?*
As a private teacher, you can give individual and/or group lessons from 20 minutes to an hour or longer. You are responsible for planning these lessons and developing an overall scheme of work for every student, using materials and repertoire suitable for different stages of musical development. In addition, you will need to arrange lesson schedules, liaise with parents, issue all invoices, collect fees and prepare and enter students for performances, auditions, festivals and examinations. The administrative aspects are time consuming but important, so it is worth setting time aside for these activities each week in order to successfully manage existing teaching and secure future work. This can include providing progress reports and feedback to parents, sending out and chasing invoices, maintaining timetables and teaching rotas as well as communicating with schools, marketing and developing new opportunities through networks and collaborations.

*Generating work*
Whether you are just starting out as a freelance instrumental teacher or establishing yourself in a new area, you will need to set about generating teaching work.
- Make sure you have an appropriate teaching space, either in your own home or in a hired studio. Do check you can use the space for business purposes.
- Promote yourself locally in music shops, local media and social media.
- Consider setting up a website, highlighting your experience, qualifications and areas of expertise.
- Join a specialist music teacher service such as **MusicTeachers.co.uk**.
- Contact local schools and offer to provide a demonstration for students or free taster lessons.

**Private/studio tuition**
**Type of employment:** you are self-employed, freelance.
**Role of the teacher:** you usually provide one-to-one tuition at home or in a private studio, or as a freelancer in schools or other settings. You generate new work for yourself. You provide performance opportunities for your students and administer all aspects of your teaching.
**Key skills:** you are required to have strong instrumental skills, be highly organised and a good communicator.

# One-to-one tuition in schools

When working in schools as a peripatetic teacher, you will potentially be responsible for arranging all aspects of your teaching, including giving demonstration lessons, negotiating your timetable around classroom activities, making exam entries and maintaining contact with parents. In some cases, instrumental teachers are invited to work alongside classroom teachers on music activities or to direct school ensembles.

As a visiting instrumental teacher (VMT) you may be employed or self-employed, and will invoice parents directly or be paid by the school, depending on the arrangement. In most cases there is an agreed hourly rate for instrumental and singing teaching (and ensemble direction) that you should clarify from the outset, along with any additional considerations such as room rent. As with private teaching, the lesson content is your responsibility, though senior members of staff, heads of department or school inspectors may observe lessons from time to time, and you may be expected to write regular progress reports and attend staff development sessions.

> **Mature learners**
> Older adults are increasingly choosing to learn an instrument as a leisure activity, and this form of teaching is potentially a valuable source of income for musicians. Teachers need to recognise and respond to the needs, aspirations and goals of these learners, which may differ from younger students. Mature learners may be more flexible if they are not restricted by working hours so can be fitted in during the week, ideal when your school students want to come for lessons after school or at the weekends.

# Online instrumental tuition

*Why teach online?*
Online tuition is a rapidly growing area of instrumental teaching and learning. Many instrumental and singing teachers have turned to online teaching as a way to continue providing tuition and earning an income when face-to-face tuition is not possible. Before the pandemic, this form of tuition was already emerging as a popular, cost-effective and practical way of teaching, especially for schools and students in rural communities where transport issues provide logistical barriers to regular peripatetic tuition. Teachers can attract students from across the globe, extending their base beyond local or national boundaries.

*Planning and preparation*
In this form of teaching, it is essential that you make every effort to simplify and streamline communication. Preparation and planning are key; elements such as teaching materials, accompaniments, lighting and repertoire should be ready before the lesson begins. Students will need to be prepared before the lesson and have a reliable instrument, music stand and other necessary equipment. They should have a quiet place for the lesson with good lighting and a reliable internet connection if possible.

The immediate nature of communication in face-to-face lessons can be impaired in online tuition and accompaniment may not be possible due to a lag in sound. You can resolve these issues by providing backing tracks or accompaniments for the student to use during lessons and the audio quality can be enhanced by using a standard conferencing microphone speaker.

*The benefits of online tuition*
These lessons can be more focussed with less potential for distraction. Whilst this can mean that the student benefits from a more intense learning experience, online lessons can be more tiring for the teacher and it is advisable to take regular breaks during teaching.

This type of tuition benefits some students as they can observe themselves as they sing or play. They can check their position and body alignment in a way that they are less likely to do in a face-to-face lesson. In addition, online lessons can be recorded by participants, with the agreement of both parties, allowing the student to benefit from repeated viewing between lessons. This also provides the teacher with an opportunity to observe their teaching and potentially improve aspects of delivery. With careful preparation, this can be a worthwhile and productive form of one-to-one instrumental tuition. Be aware that this type of tuition may not be accessible to all students due to a lack of suitable equipment/space.

*Ensembles and choirs*
During the pandemic many ensembles and choirs turned to online platforms to continue rehearsals. For many this was an entirely new venture and one that highlighted the potential for new ways of interacting and learning. Given the difficulties relating to the lag in online communication, it may not be possible for groups to rehearse in the same way as traditional ensemble rehearsal sessions. The director or lead member must remain live while the other group members mute their microphones.

This form of rehearsal can be productive, allowing focussed work on individual parts and ensuring that each participant is secure without the distraction of other musicians and background chatter. However, when each individual is muted, it is not possible to work on key aspects of ensemble playing and singing such as blend, balance and coordination. The social and interpersonal interaction that is so vital to ensemble participation for many (especially in community music making) is largely lost. Nevertheless, when necessary, online ensemble music making can help to ensure continuity and participation and connect musicians.

*Securing online teaching*

As an instrumental teacher providing online tuition, you can advertise privately and set your own hourly rates. In some cases you may be able to pay a fee to secure students via an online teaching agency and then specify the rate and all other aspects of tuition yourself. Lesson structure and content are at your discretion, along with all lesson arrangements including duration and frequency. This form of teaching, like private face-to-face tuition, features high levels of individual flexibility and autonomy and so is an attractive option for those involved in a variety of professional roles as well as teaching.

> **Top tips for successful teaching online:**
> - **Space** – make sure both you and the student are in a suitable, quiet space and make sure that the internet connection is as secure and reliable as possible.
> - **Preparation** – make sure you both have copies of all repertoire and where possible ensure that the student has a recorded accompaniment.
> - **Sound quality** – invest in a conference microphone speaker as this will enhance the sound considerably. Headphones can also help.
> - **Communication** – agree signals so that the student knows when you need them to stop playing.
> - **Expectations** – make sure the student and their parents recognise the lesson as a formal teaching arrangement and advise against the student having the lesson in their bedroom. Both you and the student should be properly dressed for the lesson.
> - **Timings** – allow at least 10 minutes between students to allow for calling, establishing connections and so on.
> - **Take breaks** – online teaching can be exhausting. Aim to have regular, longer breaks in your teaching day.

> **Online tuition**
> **Type of employment:** you are self-employed, freelance or working via an agency.
> **Role of the teacher:** you provide one-to-one instrumental tuition remotely. You plan lessons and long-term goals. You support your students' progress with appropriate repertoire and performance activities, including exams.
> **Key skills:** you need strong instrumental skills. You need to be a good communicator with an understanding of the technology involved. You must be able to adapt and develop your approach to new situations.

## Working in community music

*What is community music?*
Community music encompasses many varied forms of activity and for the musician this work represents far more than simply teaching. The term 'community music' describes music making that can be both therapeutic and educational, inclusive and accessible, with an emphasis on participation. Community musicians bridge a gap between informal music making and formal music education. It can take place in schools, hospitals, care homes, hospices, churches, prisons, rehabilitation centres, youth centres and community centres.

Participants can be of any age, and may be engaging in these activities for social reasons and to help combat issues such as loneliness, isolation, loss, illness, disability or educational difficulties. The instrumental or singing teacher as leader, facilitator, accompanist or simply as a musician can have a significant impact on the mental and physical health and well-being of the participants and as such, this is a rewarding form of work for many musicians.

*Working as a community musician*
There are various working models in community music. Self-employed, freelance work can involve agreements with specific institutions, groups or facilities where you can charge an hourly rate for rehearsals, or you could decide to establish a community group from scratch, hiring a venue and either charging a fee for participation or acquiring funding to cover costs and expenses. Alternatively, you can be employed by institutions and organisations on a more formal basis to deliver music-making activities or projects. In each of these settings, the planning needs to be carefully shaped around the needs of the participants, establishing a programme of music making that is accessible, relevant and productive for all involved.

*Preparing for specific community music contexts*
Before considering work in community music, it is important to note that expectations of music making may differ from those in formal educational contexts. Attendance and engagement can be inconsistent and as a teacher and workshop leader you should be prepared to adapt and respond to the needs, interests, goals and abilities of whoever you work with. As ever, the key to success is in the planning and preparation and in this context the ability to be responsive both personally and musically is especially important.

As an example, consider the role of teachers engaged to provide music-making activities in care homes, hospices and hospitals. In these settings it will be necessary to consider the type of repertoire and approach that might engage the participants most successfully and ensure the enjoyment of everyone involved. With this in mind, the teacher needs to provide resources that reflect the age and abilities of all and be sensitive to the style and genre that might be most accessible. Specific themes or events can work well in these situations, such as animals and pirates for children or more nostalgic material for care home residents. Key practical considerations here might include finding backing tracks or sheet music to familiar songs, developing musical activities to use in the sessions or preparing word sheets with large print. Consider a range of inclusive musical activities, such as providing some percussion instruments that are easy to hold and use. The workshop style of these sessions requires a creative and flexible approach, with a relaxed manner to music making, where you as a musician invite participants to join in, to whatever extent they are able.

Similarly, if you are planning to deliver music classes in a prison or similar institutional setting, consider the ways participants are likely to engage in this context. Group members may change from session to session and the interests and abilities of those involved will vary significantly. The participants may come from a range of cultural (and musical) backgrounds so your planning should include a variety of activities at differing levels. These should provide them with opportunities to develop their own ideas and explore musical stimuli through singing, playing, improvising, sharing or composing new material. Again, the emphasis here is on engagement in whatever way and at whatever level is most suitable and rewarding for the participants.

Settings and workplaces

> **Example: a plan for singing project in a women's open prison**
>
> *The group* — A singing group for adults from a range of backgrounds and with a mix of musical abilities.
>
> *The aim* — Social cohesion, expression, relaxation, creativity, fun.
>
> *Expectations* — A range of abilities and diverse musical tastes and interests. Participants may not attend on a regular basis, so plan for a workshop format. Have a range of strategies prepared including warm-ups and lots of potential repertoire. There may be opportunities for individuals to sing alone and/or to devise their own material.
>
> *Activities* — Fun warm-ups with relaxing breathing and posture exercises and easy vocalising, perhaps using well-known tunes in a range of styles.
>
> *Repertoire* — Take at least 7 or 8 pieces of lighter material for each session in different styles. There should be familiar music along with some lesser-known pieces, but they should always be accessible. Aim to have some part-singing or harmonies, but assess this based on the participants and make sure the focus is on fun.
>
> *Resources* — Prepare for a range of learning needs. Take word sheets with large print and some simple sheet music. Also be prepared to teach by rote (teaching people to memorise rather than reading text or music). Make the most of existing resources including a keyboard or piano and find out in advance whether it will be possible to use backing tracks.

**Working in community music**
**Type of employment:** you are self-employed, employed part-time or on an hourly basis as a freelance worker.
**Role of the teacher:** you are typically a workshop leader or ensemble director.
**Key skills:** you need strong instrumental skills. You need to have an adaptive, flexible approach, and be able to respond to situations. You should be musically resourceful, a good communicator and confident in managing varied group situations.

# Things to remember in all teaching situations

This work can vary between each of the teaching contexts described in this chapter, but there are key attributes, skills and responsibilities that apply to all teaching situations that will determine your success as a teacher. Here is a summary of the main things to consider before teaching in any setting.

- *Prepare for the teaching environment*

In every situation, consider the practical aspects of teaching in a specific environment and the expectations there might be of the teacher. It is unrealistic to expect to communicate aspects of basic technique to a large group of students without adapting the approach to the specific situation and considering the needs of all involved. Careful planning and preparation that focuses on the demands in each teaching environment are key to successful teaching.

- *Keep learning*

As musicians, we are constantly developing and adding to existing skills and abilities, whether through new repertoire or fresh challenges as performers, directors and teachers. Part of this process for you as an instrumental teacher involves exploring a wide range of resources, across various styles and genres, to engage and inspire your students. Expanding and developing your existing skills in composition, arrangement and improvisation, becoming familiar with other musical styles or learning to play another instrument are all ways in which you can improve your flexibility as a musician in teaching situations and enhance your employability.

- *Using technology as a tool*

Technology is increasingly useful as a tool in instrumental lessons. Providing accompaniments and practice resources such as recordings or recommending suitable Apps can significantly enhance the learning experience for your students. Teachers who support students in their use of technology and incorporate these tools also help students to see the value of these strategies in their practice and will increase their chances of success both as musicians and individuals.

- *Be ready for the unexpected*

Flexibility and adaptability are essential attributes in this type of work. From the student who arrives with no music having done no practice, to disruptions such as changes to venue, unexpected events will inevitably challenge even the most prepared teacher. In these situations, the experienced teacher is armed with a range of activities and strategies that they can adapt to ensure that, whatever the situation, they deliver a musically enriching experience. While it is impossible to prepare for every eventuality, it is a good idea to build a file (either physical or mental) of resources including games, exercises and repertoire that you can draw on when the unexpected interrupts the planned activities. These occasions may be challenging but they can also present an opportunity to explore ideas and have some fun!

Remember every lesson could involve that game-changing, lightbulb moment for a student. Relish and enjoy every opportunity to share your passion and skill as an instrumentalist.

**Suggested reading:**

> **The National Plan for Music Education in England**
> This is the government document that details the central strategy for schools, arts and education organisations with the aim of encouraging excellence in music education.

**Burwell, K. (2012)**, *Studio-based instrumental learning,* Farnham: Ashgate.
**Hallam, S. & Creech, A. (eds.) (2010)**, *Music education in the 21st century in the United Kingdom,* London: Institute of Education.
**Jorgensen, E. (2008)**, *The art of teaching music,* Bloomington: Indiana University Press
The new *Model Music Curriculum* has been published to support all children gain access to high-quality music education. **gov.uk**.

# 3
# Getting business ready

How often do you observe colleagues who are hugely talented as musicians and teachers but lack the practical skills to capitalise on their abilities? Successful musicians and teachers need a working knowledge of contracts and finance *as well as* musicianship skills and an enthusiasm for teaching and performing. Mastering the ability to promote yourself and your business successfully is not in conflict with 'art' – in fact, it will ultimately leave you free to focus more of your energies on the creativity at the heart of your practice. This chapter will take you through the basics of **employment law**, **contracts**, **finance** and **self-promotion** to help you 'get business ready'.

## The different types of employment status

*Why do you need to know about employment status?*
Employment status relates to various rights, responsibilities, entitlements and benefits at work. Musicians who teach often work under a variety of contracts. They may be unaware of exactly how they are engaged until an issue arises and it comes to light that the wrong employment status has been used. This could mean that they miss out on their legal entitlements.

It is important to recognise the difference in terms, conditions and rights applied to the three different employment statuses of '**employed**', '**worker**' (often used interchangeably with 'zero-hour') and '**self-employed**', as this will have a direct effect on your working life. Two helpful sources of information here are the government's website (**gov.uk**) and the Advisory Conciliation and Arbitration Services' website (**acas.org.uk**). ACAS is a government-funded independent organisation that provides assistance with employment issues and workplace mediation and is a valuable source of advice and guidance for many workplace issues.

Most musicians who teach are either wholly self-employed or combine self-employment with employed or zero-hour work. Full-time employed roles for musicians as teachers are relatively rare and limited mainly to the independent sector, music services or other educational institutions, although music services are increasingly employing their teachers part-time, using zero-hour worker or self-employed agreements.

*Employee*

You are an **employee** if:
- you have an employment contract
- you have regular work provided by your employer
- you are employed to do the work personally
- you must do the work as outlined in the contract

Your **employment rights** include:
- written terms (a 'written statement of employment particulars') outlining your job rights and responsibilities, as a minimum
- sick, holiday and parental leave pay
- being able to claim redundancy or unfair dismissal after two years' service
- National Minimum Wage
- payslips
- protection against unlawful discrimination
- protection for whistleblowing
- not being treated unfairly if you work part time

*Worker*

A worker's employment is more casual, often on a 'zero hour' or 'as and when' basis. If you are a **worker**, you should:
- have a 'contract for services', which can be verbal or written, detailing the work you have agreed to do and the pay you will receive
- be employed to do the work personally
- have no obligation to accept work, but you should do any work that has been agreed

As a worker, you have **employment rights** including:
- written terms outlining your job rights and responsibilities
- paid holiday or holiday pay
- National Minimum Wage
- payslips
- protection against unlawful discrimination
- protection for whistleblowing
- not being treated unfairly if you work part-time

*Self-employed*

You are **self-employed** if you:
- are responsible for how and when you work
- are the owner of a company or are a freelancer
- invoice for your pay
- get contracts to provide services for clients
- are able to send someone else to do the work for you, if appropriate
- are able to work for different clients and charge different fees
- do not get paid holiday or sick leave

Despite not having an employer, you do still have **rights**, including:
- protection for your health and safety on a client's premises
- protection against discrimination

# Who decides my employment status?

Here are three scenarios, each describing someone who has just been engaged by a school as a visiting instrumental or singing teacher. Which one represents the way employment status should be decided?

**1**

*'The head of music called and told me I could either go on the payroll as an employed teacher or be self-employed. It's up to me, depending on whether I want tax deducted at source or prefer to self-assess my tax. The work is the same either way.'*

**2**

*'The head of music called and told me that the school does a self-employed agreement with its visiting instrumental or singing teachers. We get paid a certain fee and we have to invoice at a certain time. They don't like us using deputies but we can if we really need to, up to twice a term.'*

**3**

*'The head of music called and explained how teaching at the school works. They like teachers to be consistent, only using deputies when absolutely needed, and the rate of pay is agreed each year by the board of governors. Overall, they need more control over the teachers than a self-employed agreement would allow, so we are workers with tax deducted at source.'*

**Scenario 1** is the most dubious as it presents employment status as a matter of free choice, to be decided on the basis of how the teacher would like to pay tax.

**Scenario 2** is potentially legitimate, although the school seems to be dictating quite a lot: the fee, when invoices should be submitted, when deputies (deps) can be used. A self-employed teacher should be able to negotiate their own fee, invoice when they want within reason, and use deps reasonably as and when. If these clarifications can be made through dialogue, this would be an acceptable way to define and agree self-employed status.

**Scenario 3** is the most legitimate. The school explains that the teachers' pattern of work aligns with worker status rather than self-employed status. This does not mean that other employment issues may not arise – for example, holiday pay has not been mentioned, but the basic premise is sound.

The most important thing to remember is that employment status is not something that should be chosen by the employer or the worker. Rather, it is decided by the pattern of work. Control versus flexibility is the defining variable of the different employment statuses, as this diagram shows:

**Control:** full employment rights          **Flexibility:** minimal employment rights

| Employed | Worker | Self-employed |
| --- | --- | --- |
| Employer has maximum control, dictating pay and patterns of work. In return, employee receives maximum benefits of employment. | Employer has some control, dictating pay, but worker can accept or decline work. In return, worker receives some benefits of employment. | Self-employed person is free to set rates and working arrangements. In return, client (e.g. school) offers minimal employment benefits. |

# What if my employment status seems wrong?

Imagine you are told by a school that you will be self-employed but that the school will fix the rate and control you in other ways that feel more like employment. What should you do? If you feel able, raise the issue with your point of contact at the school, or with the human resources manager. Hopefully you will be able to have a reasonable discussion about your concerns, but if not, contact a trade union, such as the Musicians' Union, who will be able to advise and can support you by mediating with the school if appropriate (as long as you are a member, of course). If this fails, the ultimate legal recourse is to pursue a claim at an employment tribunal, but due to the drawn-out nature and expense of the process, this is usually to be avoided unless there is no alternative.

Employment law and tax law change regularly and sometimes there is conflicting guidance as to whether work is considered employed or self-employed. Her Majesty's Revenue and Customs (HMRC) are able to investigate the status of work completed by individuals for institutions and assess whether they are genuinely self-employed. They will examine the indicators of how individuals are paid to ensure that employers are not avoiding giving contracts for work that is considered to be employed. It is your responsibility to keep up to date with changes in the law surrounding employment and tax and to ensure that you are being compliant as far as you possibly can. It is tempting to accept any work that is available at the start of your career but you do need to be professional in knowing what the implications could be. If you have concerns it is best to get advice and guidance before signing contracts or agreeing terms and conditions.

# Getting paid

*Employed*
If you are employed by an institution or organisation then your hourly rate of pay is usually set by them and will be fixed on a pay scale. There is usually no room for negotiation on this unless you are able to offer more or you have specific skills that they need. Do ask what the rate of pay is and what it includes (such as holiday pay). Your hourly rate will probably be the gross rate of pay which includes all benefits but without any deductions taken off. If you are employed on 'Pay As You Earn' then tax and national insurance will be deducted from your earnings. Again it is worth checking to make sure you are clear what hourly rate you are expecting. Employers make additional contributions for National Insurance and pension, so these hourly rates are usually lower than self-employed rates.

*Self-employed*

If you are truly self-employed then you should set your own hourly rates of pay or fees for whatever work you are doing. Sometimes organisations or institutions will say that the self-employed rate is fixed or may 'recommend' a rate, but this can be challenged as setting your own rate of pay is one of the indicators of being self-employed.

## How to set your own rates

The Musicians' Union publish their recommended hourly teaching rates annually for the new academic year (available at **themu.org**). These are based pro rata on the Statutory Teachers' Pay and Conditions scales. The rates are revised each year and adjusted accordingly based on the inflation rate. These are recommended minimums, and a good starting point for pitching your own rates. It is useful to take into account what the local market is, what you are offering and what your skills and experience are.

Be realistic about what you charge but take into account where you are based in the country (cities often have higher rates than more rural locations) and if you are teaching from your own home or travelling to students' houses, which will always take longer. You can be creative in your pricing by offering discounts for lessons paid in advance, holding a taster lesson that is reimbursed if a course of lessons is taken up afterwards or offering discounts for families and friends. Think of how you can provide more services for parents such as obtaining music or entering students for exams, which will justify a higher hourly rate.

Have a policy on cancellations and whether a student will be charged. It is important that you are strict enough to ensure cancellations don't become commonplace as this will affect your income, but have some flexibility so that it isn't too onerous for those paying the bill!

Having an hourly rate that you feel reflects your expertise will help if you are asked to do work that involves teaching groups, directing ensembles or taking a workshop, as you can evaluate how much extra work or preparation time that will involve. Remember that out of your hourly rate of pay comes your tax and National Insurance as well as your pension contributions and money to cover time taken off for holiday or illness.

For private tuition, communicate effectively with your students and whoever is paying for the lessons about how much you charge, what that includes and when any fee increases will take place. Give as much notice as you can and aim to increase at a set time each year as this will help people budget for the music lessons.

Be efficient and timely about invoicing and make sure you chase payments so they avoid becoming bad debts. The MU will follow up unpaid invoices on your behalf if you are a member and usually an official letter from them will encourage people to pay, however they will also go to the small claims court on your behalf if needed.

# Holiday pay

Employees and workers are both entitled to paid leave that is either calculated as a number of days per year or, for those working on hourly contracts, as an added percentage on the hourly rate. In the UK, the Working Time Regulations that govern our employment law state that full-time employees are entitled to 5.6 weeks' paid holiday per year, with part-time employees getting a pro rata equivalent.

If you are not given paid days off as part of your role, you should be receiving holiday pay, which your employer is legally obliged to calculate and explain to you.

*How holiday pay is calculated*
Holiday pay should be itemised as a minimum additional 12.07% on top of the hourly teaching rate.

> **Example**
> If your hourly rate is £35, your rate including holiday pay will be £39.22.
> £35 x 1.1207 = £39.2245

The 12.07% is arrived at by taking the 5.6 weeks of the year that are not worked from 52 weeks to give a working year of 46.4 weeks. 46.4 weeks is divided by 5.6 to get 12.07.

Since 2019 there has been some dispute about the 12.07% calculation driven by case law that may mean you are entitled to more holiday pay than before. Therefore 12.07% of your hourly rate is the absolute minimum you should receive as holiday pay.

> Self-employed people do not get paid holiday. If you are self-employed you should ideally include in your rate an amount that can be set aside for when you take time off.

*What if my holiday pay seems wrong?*
By far the most common issue raised by musicians who teach relates to holiday pay not being paid at all, rather than disagreements over the percentage. Sometimes employers will claim that the hourly rate they offer includes holiday pay, but this is dubious if they did not communicate this clearly at the outset. Contact your Trade Union if this is the case, as they are able to investigate and advise if holiday pay has not been paid correctly. They are also able to follow up with employers to ensure that the correct hourly rate is paid, and in some cases secure 'back' holiday pay.

It is illegal to have 'rolled-up' holiday pay in one hourly rate. It must state on a payslip or in a contract how it has been calculated, and it is completely reasonable to challenge your employer if this is not clear.

## Am I getting all my employment benefits?

If you are working under an employment contract then you are entitled to a range of benefits. Some of them are your legal right and some of them will be contractual.

For **employees**, check:
- What is your employer's **sick pay** and **parental/adoption leave** policy? Both of these have statutory minimums, but many employers offer enhanced provisions that should be specified in your contract.
- Likewise, **redundancy** (should this arise) is governed by statutory minimum payments, but your employer may offer an enhanced redundancy policy.

For **employees** and **workers**, check:
- Are you getting regular payslips with **holiday pay, tax** and any **pension contributions** clearly itemised? You are entitled to these and knowing what you are getting each month should help you keep tabs on your benefits.
- You may be entitled to a workplace pension if you earn more than a certain amount. This should be specified in your contract or statement of particulars.

## School teachers' pay and conditions (STPC) and zero-hour contracts

Classroom teachers are often on school teachers' pay and conditions (STPC) – an enhanced set of benefits negotiated over many years by teaching unions. It is primarily for those who work as classroom teachers on a full-time or fixed-hours part-time basis, therefore if you find yourself doing regular classroom or large-group teaching, it might be worth speaking to your employer about whether you are eligible for STPC. To access the higher pay bands within STPC it is often necessary to have Qualified Teacher Status (QTS) obtained through taking a Postgraduate Qualification in Education (PGCE), and an employer may even support you in working towards this.

At the other end of the scale is the zero-hour contract, which is the arrangement for many musicians who teach. The zero-hour contract offers the flexibility for casual workers to accept or turn down shifts as they like. The difficulty comes when it is applied to teaching work. Employers might argue that they use zero-hour contracts to allow teachers to choose whether they take on particular students or schools. The reality, though, is that once teachers have accepted a piece of work, they are often committed to it. Even if their agreement states that they can review their teaching commitment each term, in practice it is awkward to abandon students, and it may also be frowned on by the employer. This contractual relationship may in fact be closer to employment than worker status. There may be increased scrutiny on zero-hour contracts in the future as workplace disputes reach employment tribunals and judgements are translated into case law.

## Contracts

Having contracts for your work is vital. Whenever there is a business or workplace conflict to resolve, by far the easiest way to do this is to go back to your contract and check what it says. However, many instrumental and singing teachers operate without any written contract or agreement in place or are working under contracts that have never been updated or are not fit for purpose. The reality of the situation only comes to light when there is a dispute between the teacher and engager, such as when claiming fees for cancelled lessons, or trying to clarify a school's sick pay policy. It is beneficial for both parties to have a clear contract in place to cover the obligations of each party and include important matters such as notice periods. Always ask for a contract for whatever work you are being offered and if possible, have it checked by a lawyer before you sign it.

> **MU contract checking service**
> The MU provides a checking service that allows members to send in contracts to be reviewed by specialist lawyers through its Contract Advisory Service and Employment Contract Advisory Service. The legal team will provide appropriate advice and guidance on any contract related to your professional work.

If you are working on a self-employed basis it is also advisable to have contracts in place for all your teaching work, whether for private individual students, for work in schools and institutions or for workshops and ensembles. If you are not offered a contract then use a template or devise your own to ensure that if there is a dispute then both sides have a document to refer to.

> **Contract templates**
> The Musicians' Union has a number of teaching contracts available for its members to download. These include contracts for:
> - Private teaching – for the provision of private music lessons.
> - Teaching in schools – for work in schools as a self-employed teacher, paid for by the school.
> - Private teaching in schools – for work in schools, paid for by the parent.
> - Online teaching contract for under 18s.
> - Online teaching contract for over 18s.

## Teaching for agencies and other organisations

*Teaching agencies*
Teaching agencies for instrumental and singing teachers are prolific and many musicians sign up when trying to build a teaching practice. Generally, agencies operate by introducing students to a teacher and taking an introductory fee, or the agency is paid a percentage of the teachers' hourly rate. Most teachers using an agency will be self-employed and therefore responsible for their own tax and national insurance, although occasionally the work will be employed or on a zero-hours contract. Some agencies may provide other services such as invoicing, collecting fees and marketing, which may work well for some teachers. Be aware that these extra services will have cost implications.

Check any contract provided by a teaching agency before agreeing to its terms and conditions as some clauses maybe onerous. If you want to leave the agency, you will probably be unable to take your students with you without breaching the terms of the contract.

*Music teacher co-operatives*
Music teacher co-operatives are set up and run *for* and *by* its members. They provide a mechanism for sharing ideas, costs, resources, skills and expertise and are governed by a set of shared values. Teachers working for a co-operative can be either self-employed or employed but their aim is always to provide support for each other. There are a number of successful co-operatives for music teachers based around the UK.

*Community interest companies*
Community interest companies (CICs) are designed as social enterprises that use their profits and assets for the public good. CICs must be registered as limited companies. They may provide tuition in formal or non-formal settings.

*Music service trusts*
Music service trusts are 'not-for-profit' organisations and a number of them have been set up to provide tuition in schools, sometimes in areas when the Local Authority music service has ceased to exist.

*Licensed teacher schemes*
An area may have 'Licensed' or 'Associate' teacher schemes where schools are able to recruit their instrumental and vocal teachers from a recognised register. These might simply be a list of teachers' contact details for schools to use, although some will want DBS (Disclosure and Barring Service) information and you will have to go through an approval process before you can be included.

# Self-promotion

To build a successful teaching practice you will need to be to consistent and diligent in your efforts to promote and market yourself. There are many listing websites you can use (some paid, some free) and there are other avenues you can explore to reach out to more students. Do not underestimate the power of word of mouth, as parents and students will be your best advocates in recommending you to others. Consider what you think students (and parents) want from a teacher and then hone your skills to match their expectations.

If you want to develop work in schools, offer to lead workshops or demonstrations to attract more students and take all opportunities to be involved in local musical activities, including amateur music making. Look at connecting with a music shop to supply instruments and printed music or offer trial lessons or vouchers for lessons that can be purchased as gifts. Be creative and resourceful in building up your student base until ideally you are able to create a waiting list where you have more students than you can accommodate.

*Using social media for promotion*
You may consider putting together your own website to promote yourself, whether as a musician or a teacher. Social media can be a useful tool for instrumental teachers, offering a convenient way to advertise and generate new students. Parents commonly look for teachers by searching online, so a presence here is as important as local advertising through schools and local media.

If you are planning to use social media, consider the platform that is most appropriate for the job. Both Facebook and Twitter are well suited to promoting specific activities, events or services and can offer the opportunity to link to other aspects of your professional portfolio, such as performance work.

It will help to have a consistent image across all advertising, promotional materials and platforms. This might sound excessive when you are simply promoting yourself as a teacher, but will help to convey a professional approach and potentially give you an edge over the competition.

*Maintaining a professional profile*
Social media is a public space and, if you have a public page, all interactions can be seen by anyone else. With this in mind, be careful about who you choose to follow as you may inadvertently share material, ideas or images which are not appropriate or complementary to your professional image. It is a good idea to have completely separate work and personal social media pages, to protect your image and avoid sharing personal information. Similarly, while you may want to encourage followers, it is important to maintain a professional profile and avoid following students.

Be mindful of your privacy and avoid sharing personal details that are not strictly necessary, such as your address. You should also avoid sharing or posting pictures, recordings or details about individual students unless you have the explicit consent of the student and parent.

**Top tips for using social media:**
- Post regularly.
- Update followers on tuition offers, practice tips, mini warm-ups, cool downs, exercises, teaching ideas and recordings of recommended repertoire for students.
- Include links to events.
- Show excerpts of your own performances where possible to enhance your appeal as a practising musician.
- Convey both your skill and passion for teaching with potential students.
- Keep your personal and professional pages separate.
- Don't link to personal pages, or include personal details such as your address.
- Use the right platform for the job.
- Present a consistent image and message.
- Don't follow or 'friend' students.
- Do be aware that all interactions can be seen and be careful about who you choose to follow.
- Don't post pictures or recordings that feature students unless you have consent from the student and parent.

# Finance

If you are starting out as a freelance musician undertaking a variety of work, including teaching, then you must register with **Her Majesty's Revenue and Customs (HMRC)** as being self-employed. Failure to do so can incur a penalty. Most musicians who teach will in reality do a mixture of employed and self-employed work and it is worthwhile finding out about any potential tax saving opportunities regarding traded income through claiming expenses against self-employed income.

If some of your work is employed and some self-employed then the tax rate you pay should work out the same overall. The only difference is that in employed work tax is usually taken at source through PAYE (Pay As You Earn) schemes.

Many freelance musicians will do their own accounts and work out their own tax liability but to start with you can always engage an accountant to advise. They will also be able to explain what you are eligible to claim as legitimate expenses, saving you money, so are worth the investment.

## Insurances

If you are working as a freelance musician with a portfolio career that includes teaching, then it is worth being insured for every situation in which you work. If you are employed by an organisation or institution then they should have **Employer's Liability Insurance** in place. You may be covered by the building you work in to some extent, so it is always worth checking what you are covered for and what you are responsible for. If you are self-employed then having the correct insurances in place is your responsibility.

It is recommended that you have **Public and Products Liability Insurance** to cover for legal liability for damages following injury to a third party (not an employee) or damage to property whilst performing or teaching. Often engagers will ask to see evidence of this cover before work is offered.

**Professional Indemnity Insurance** is also a useful insurance to have as a teacher as this protects you against legal liability claims resulting in errors and omissions arising from the teaching or lecturing of music. Increasingly engagers may want to see evidence of this cover being in place before offering work.

Other insurances worth considering include **Tax Investigation Insurance** to cover any professional fees of a tax or VAT investigation and **Personal Accident Cover** or **Critical Health Cover**, which will cover you if you are unable to work because of an accident or illness. These are important issues to consider if you are self-employed and not eligible for benefits. It is also really important to ensure that your instruments and related equipment are properly insured if you are using them for teaching so you are covered if they are damaged or stolen.

> See page 44 for details of the Musicians' Union insurance packages.

## The benefits of joining a trade union

As a teacher working in the music education sector it is advisable that you join a trade union that is appropriate to your work. Trade unions are there to provide advice and guidance for all your work as well as the benefits required by a self-employed individual, such as insurances. Trade unions will also represent you in meetings if needed and will provide legal advice on a variety of issues. All of these would be very costly to source and fund by yourself.

Deciding which trade union to join will depend on what work you undertake. If you are a musician working in a portfolio career that includes teaching, then the **Musicians' Union** is the most suitable as it represents 32,000 professional musicians working across the whole of the music industry. About two thirds of its members work in the music education sector. The MU also has partnerships and joint membership arrangements with other Trade Unions to ensure that all your educational work is covered.

*Partner trade unions working with the Musicians' Union*
The **National Education Union (NEU)** is for school teachers, further education lecturers, educational support staff and teaching assistants. It has over 500,000 members and is the largest education union in the UK. neu.org

The **University and College Union (UCU)** represents over 120,000 academics and support staff working in Further and Higher Educational institutions. ucu.org

The **Educational Institution Scotland (EIS)** is the oldest teachers' trade union in the world, having been founded in 1847. It represents over 54,000 teachers and lecturers working in the Scottish education system. eis.org

**Musicians' Union**
#behindeverymusician

The MU is the ideal organisation to join if you are a musician with a portfolio career that includes work in the education sector. It has a package of benefits and services that are designed to support those working as musicians as well as specialist officials who are able to advise you on specific issues that you may face whilst teaching.

**Benefits include:**
- Comprehensive packages of insurances including £10 million of Public Liability; £2000 instrument cover; personal accident cover; professional indemnity insurance for those working in education and professional expenses cover for any investigation by the tax authorities.
- Legal advice and assistance on all aspects of your career as a musician including employment, contract, copyright and intellectual property law.
- Access to help and advice on a range of issues from Health and Safety to working with other musicians; from hearing damage to unpaid fees.
- Free training, events, workshops, networking and career advice.

The MU also lobbies on behalf of its members to ensure that their interests are represented on a local, national and international level. It works with other unions through the Trade Union Council (TUC) and the Federation of Entertainment Unions (FEU) to secure improvements for the working lives of musicians. As a member of UK Music, the major lobbying organisation representing the music industry, and the Federation for International Musicians (FIM), it gives voice to its members both nationally and internationally.

themu.org

# 4

# What is good teaching?

Understandings of effective instrumental and singing teaching will vary according to the individual teacher, student and perhaps instrument, but there are common questions and issues which are relevant to all.

- What are the main goals?
- What does progress look like?
- How can we plan effectively for lessons and what should that planning look like?
- What are the most common strategies used by instrumental and singing teachers?
- How does the role of the student change as they grow older and develop technical skills?

This chapter will explore some of these key questions and provide some ideas to help instrumental and singing teachers develop an approach that puts the student at the centre.

## What is the main purpose of learning music?

Learning to play an instrument or learning to sing is itself a rewarding and fulfilling activity, but it also has cognitive, emotional and developmental benefits for the individual that are valuable whatever their age. Learning to play or sing can help improve reading ability, memory, speech-fluency, problem-solving skills and reasoning as well as time management, team working, social skills and the ability to handle stress. For younger students these benefits can enhance overall progress in education, while for more mature individuals, music making is a valuable way of maintaining both cognitive functions and general well-being.

## Planning for lessons

So how do we plan for instrumental music lessons? All learning activities work best when there is a clear sense of purpose and well-defined expectations. The student should know what is expected of them as well as what they can expect from the teacher. One of your roles as a teacher is to establish goals and expectations as part of an ongoing learning process with a student or group of students. This form of relationship requires the teacher to be pro-active rather than having a responsive, 'what did you do this week?' attitude to lessons. Planning is key and the adage 'fail to prepare, prepare to fail' is especially relevant to instrumental and singing teaching, where progress can depend on suitable repertoire along with setting appropriate practice goals and strategies.

Planning can (and should) include short-term and long-term goals for each student or group as well as aims for activities in specific weekly sessions. The important thing is to identify overall aims for the learner and ensure that each lesson contributes in some way towards reaching these goals.

### Lesson plans

Some schools and music services encourage plans for instrumental lessons. This can be complex as your students may arrive without an instrument or music; they may not have practised or have regular access to an instrument on which to practise. Despite these problems, it is still a very good idea to have a clearly defined plan for each student or group for each term, detailing agreed goals and specific repertoire along with weekly notes to record progress in each lesson along with specific practice targets for the following session.

This can be especially useful if you are working with lots of students in a variety of settings. It helps to maintain a pro-active approach to teaching and provides a ready source of information that you can draw on for reports and feedback to parents and carers.

Students should be encouraged to keep notes to remind them of specific activities and suggestions from the lesson along with agreed areas for practice and relevant practice strategies. This approach will ensure that students, along with their parents or carers, have a clear understanding of the requirements. Practice diaries are useful and readily available from music suppliers.

## TERMLY LESSON NOTES FOR TEACHERS

| Student/group/ensemble | | Term | |
|---|---|---|---|
| **Agreed objectives for this term** (agreed with student at the start of each term) | | | |
| **Agreed objectives for the year** (agreed with student at the start of each year) | | | |

| Date | Lesson activities | Agreed practice activities |
|---|---|---|
| | | |
| | | |
| | | |
| | | |
| | | |
| | | |
| | | |
| | | |
| | | |
| | | |
| | | |
| | | |
| | | |

## Communication with parents and carers

The role of the parent is vitally important in supporting the student and helping to establish effective practice habits, especially in the early stages of instrumental study. Communication between teacher and parent is therefore central to the learning process, whether through the student notebook, or via email and telephone conversations. Parents and carers can report practice activities and work with the teacher to provide a support system through which the student is able to progress. At the very least, you should provide regular feedback to parents and carers and highlight any problems such as a lack of practice, an apparent loss of motivation or non-attendance at lessons as soon as they emerge. In many cases the school or music service will require teachers to provide progress reports. Where this is not the case, you might consider communicating feedback to parents and carers at the end of each term and checking on practice behaviour between lessons.

---

**TERMLY PROGRESS REPORT**

**Name of student:**           **Term:**

**Teacher's comments:**

To include key areas such as technique, musicianship and practice, along with progress towards specific goals. Also outline areas for further development.

**Student's comments:**

Encourage the student to reflect on progress made this term and areas where they feel they can improve.

**Parent/carer's comments:**

**Teacher's signature:**           **Parent's signature:**

## Taking on students from other teachers

It is inevitable that students will change teachers at different points in their development, whether this is because of a change in schools, relocation, for reasons relating to progression or other circumstances. In the first encounters with a transferred student, you can usefully aim to acknowledge and build on what the student has already achieved in a positive and supportive way. Teaching styles may vary and we may have differing priorities and approaches as individuals, but you can reinforce the sense of learning as a process if you stress that you are building on what they already know. This in turn can help the student to appreciate all learning as intrinsically useful rather than developing a dependency on an individual teacher. When the student eventually moves on to a different teacher, you can support them by encouraging them to be open-minded and accepting of new ideas. This can help in easing important transitions and again foster an understanding of the process in which the activity itself is more important for the student that any single teacher or institution.

## How structured should lessons be?

Every student is unique and a 'one size fits all' approach can easily deter some otherwise keen musicians. Traditional models of instrumental and singing lessons that start with scales or studies and progress to repertoire selected by the teacher may still be relevant for some students, but this approach will not match the interests and aspirations of all budding musicians. Consider the student's goals, interests and rate of progress when planning a range of musically engaging activities.

If you, as the teacher, actively encourage the student to explore material they enjoy, they will be more likely to find the activity rewarding and want to practise more. You can lead students from familiar to less-familiar styles and encourage them to express themselves through music, making links and approaching music making with an open and creative mind. The key thing to remember here is to **teach the student, not the instrument!**

## Key lesson components

Whatever the instrument or age of the student, there are key features that can be included in every lesson. Activities to improve and develop aspects of technique and communication along with exercises to nurture musicianship and creativity are essential in the development of musical skill.

> **Key lesson components include:**
> **Warm-up and cool down:** instrument-specific exercises to help avoid strain and injury.
> **Aspects of technique:** posture, embouchure, hand position, breath control, etc.
> **Creative work:** improvisation, composition.
> **Repertoire:** exploring new material and technical elements of existing pieces.

In his *Simultaneous Learning* approach, educationalist Paul Harris suggests four basic principles that should feature in all instrumental teaching and learning from the earliest stages – the four Ps: **posture, pulse, phonology** and **personality**. Harris argues that musical encounters that feature all of these elements provide a rounded experience that can result in musical fulfilment for the student, whatever their goals (**Harris, 2014**, *Simultaneous learning: the definitive guide*, p.37).

It may be that you include posture, pulse and phonology as part of a technical warm up that is related to specific aspects of repertoire in the lesson, or that elements of style and character (personality) connect technical work to a particular period, genre or piece. However you approach these principals, aim to explore them in each lesson.

# The importance of warm-ups

All instrumental and singing lessons should begin with a warm-up to prepare the body for efficient and effective activity and to minimise the risk of injury. The key functions of warm-ups are to:
- prepare the body
- set the tone and atmosphere for the lesson
- introduce key elements of the lesson
- introduce new aspects of technique
- prevent injury
- establish safe and effective practice habits

Warming up allows the student to ease into the lesson and provides an opportunity to establish, develop and reinforce aspects of technique including posture, breathing, embouchure and tone. Select a warm-up appropriate for the ability of the student and the activities planned for the main body of the lesson.

# Developing aural skills

Developing aural skills in young musicians can increase confidence, enhance creativity and improve their abilities relating to pitch, rhythm and pulse. Professional musicians use aural skills whether they are involved in teaching, performance, community music or music therapy, so it makes sense to build the development of aural skills into your instrumental lessons in a practical way.

Consider the following strategies:
- Play a pattern; the student plays it back. Increase the length and complexity of the pattern.
- Play through a short piece that the student is working on and change specific elements, then ask the student to identify the changes. Try it the other way around.
- Play a well-known tune and then provide the first note for the student. Ask the student to work out the tune and then play by ear while you play an accompaniment.
- Play a well-known tune and stop at random points. Ask the student to finish the phrase by singing, clapping or playing on their instrument, depending on ability.

*Call and response*
Use call and response from the very earliest stages in tuition, either between teacher and student or between students in a group, to bring a real sense of fun to aural training. You could begin with simple rhythmic patterns, progressing to short melodies using two or three notes. Call and response can be used as a warm-up to introduce patterns from new repertoire, and can be treated as a game, especially in group situations. As the student advances, it can be used as a strategy when working on specific styles of articulation and phrasing and can help to develop confidence in improvisation.

# How do instrumental and singing teachers teach?

Instrumental and singing teachers use a range of strategies and are generally actively involved in demonstrating and assisting the student, especially in the early stages of tuition. The role of the teacher also involves helping the student to develop effective practice strategies and habits including problem-solving techniques that allow them to become a more independent learner. Here are some of the most common strategies.

*Scaffolding*
In the context of instrumental teaching and learning, scaffolding refers to the way in which the teacher supports the student by playing, singing or clapping along with them as they play, often playing along on the same instrument or at the piano. Scaffolding can help maintain pulse, provide a clear melodic line for the student to follow and highlight musical elements such as phrasing, articulation and dynamics. In time, the teacher might reduce the level of scaffolding as the student becomes more confident, perhaps playing more quietly or only joining in where support is required.

Scaffolding is a useful strategy with beginners and younger students and in cases where students are lacking in confidence to ease the tension and reduce the extent to which students feel exposed when playing alone. It is, however, vitally important that students eventually become accustomed to playing and singing without this support and the teacher should always focus on the posture, confidence and sound of the student during the scaffolding process.

*Modelling*
In this form of support, teachers provide a model that the student can observe and apply in their own playing. It is used with students at every level in combination with other strategies. Instrumental and singing teachers use modelling as a way to communicate various musical and technical elements, from effective posture, hand position or bowing to phrasing, articulation, pronunciation and dynamics. The teacher might model a specific rhythmic feature that the student is finding problematic or introduce new fingering. This is also an effective way to demonstrate aspects of style and character that might be unfamiliar to the student. Typically, the teacher models and the student follows, though in group lessons a student may model to the rest of the group.

Modelling should not replace the independent learning of the student and each learner should be encouraged to develop and enjoy their own sound rather than copying the teacher or any one specific artist. This is especially important for singers where attempts to mimic other voices can lead to a range of vocal problems.

*Imagery and analogy*
When introducing technical aspects or musical ideas to students, especially younger students, teachers often use imagery and analogy to help make them more accessible. There are multiple examples of this approach for each discipline; consider the various ways in which string teachers help young students to understand bow hold or the range of explanations for hand position and posture at the piano. Singing teachers commonly employ imagery to help the student with tone production, for example imagining a hooting owl to help connect to the diaphragm and reproducing a gasp of surprise to lift the soft palate.

Teachers and directors will also use more identifiable images or concepts to help advanced students and ensembles connect with a musical idea. Imagine an orchestral conductor encouraging the upper strings to shimmer like *the wind through a field of long grass* or a choral conductor suggesting that *piano* should have as much intensity as the loudest *forte* but *from the other side of a closed door*.

The development of shared understanding through imagery and analogy is a common and effective tool in music education and contributes to our shared language as musicians. We learn to interpret expressions such as 'I'll give you two bars in' in particular ways and in doing so we share in a divergence of meaning where a specific understanding is associated with otherwise common phrases, actions or items. Imagery and analogy are central to the intersubjectivity of musicians, where for example the instruction 'disney princess' might remind a singer or group of singers to adopt a specific style of singing or 'spider!' might prompt a piano student to consider their hand position as they play. These are shared during the process of instrumental teaching as part of the students' introduction to the language and culture of music and musicians. Individual teachers and directors commonly devise their own imagery and analogy. This can be an ongoing process in which teachers look for new ways to communicate concepts, techniques or ideas to students that are relevant to the age, interests and abilities of the student.

Instrumental and singing lessons typically include all of these strategies in combination and teachers usually develop their own mix of scaffolding and modelling to suit students at different ages and stages of development. When working with younger students, you might use all of these strategies, while older and more advanced students usually require less scaffolding. Whatever the lesson or instrument, be aware of the needs of each student and adopt the most appropriate strategy.

# The development of metacognitive skills

One of the most important aspects of tuition for the instrumental or singing teacher is the development of appropriate learning and practice behaviours in the student. When learning to play an instrument, the student is required to spend significant amounts of time working alone, so they need to understand how to work and learn independently. This in turn requires metacognitive skills ranging from specific practice strategies and techniques to time management and problem-solving. To help in the development of these skills, the teacher can model the problem-solving process in lessons, for example by demonstrating how to work out areas of fingering or bowing, and encouraging the student to demonstrate and explain these and other aspects of technique. If the teacher only demonstrates and provides answers in lessons, the student is unlikely to develop problem-solving abilities. Ideally, the teacher will scaffold the student in their problem solving by asking questions and providing hints and suggestions that help them to discover solutions themselves.

*Conversations about practice*
From an early stage, students understand that progress involves working towards a level of tone and fluency on their chosen instrument. It is important to make sure that students also make the connection between regular practice and progress. Conversations about practice can be very useful in understanding ways to support the student. Asking *how, where, what*, rather than simply *how often* can help the teacher adapt goals and potentially identify ways to provide specific support.

*Asking questions*
Starting the lesson with questions about practice highs and lows can engage the student and encourage them to reflect on progress from their perspective. This approach can be used throughout the lesson to check on understanding and to encourage the student to actively reflect on their playing rather than simply responding to feedback. This in turn can help students to become more effective independent learners.

From the earliest stages of tuition, you can help develop students' problem-solving strategies and encourage them to identify and tackle difficult aspects of their playing through questions and prompts.

The following questions are useful starters:

*Talking about practice*
How did your practice go this week?
Where do you feel you made the most progress?
Did you have any problems?
Is there anything you want to go over?
Shall we make a plan for the next week?

*Talking about repertoire*
What do you like about playing this piece?
Which is the most difficult part? Why? How can we tackle that?
What did you think of that? What went well?
Which part of that could you improve? How?
What other music does this piece remind you of?
What do you think this piece is about? How could you express that?
How can you improve this piece now?
How can you practise this section/pattern?

Questions that prompt students to reflect on their playing, identifying mistakes and suggesting solutions are especially useful in encouraging independent practice skills and this in turn can affect motivation and progress. This approach will help to develop skills that can be applied not just in instrumental playing but in all learning situations.

## Age, learning development and motivation

Teaching the *student* rather than the *instrument* involves understanding the way in which learners at different ages and stages engage and respond and using the teaching approach that best supports and motivates each individual.

*Stages in the development of practical skills*
**Motor stage** – the learner understands what is required and practical activities are carried out while consciously thinking through each step.

**Associative stage** – the learner begins to put together sequences and patterns and solve problems, becoming more fluent over time. Mistakes can be identified and corrected.

**Autonomous stage** – practical skills become automated and can be carried out without conscious effort. Skills develop and improve each time they are used, building in speed and fluency.

*Motivation*
While younger students can be motivated to practise through rewards, praise and encouragement from parents, carers and teachers, more advanced students are ideally more independent in their practice habits, motivated by their own internal goals rather than external rewards.

There are various theories of motivation that can be applied to instrumental teaching and learning and provide insight into the motivation to perform specific activities.

**Expectancy value theory** suggests that individuals will invest in a particular task if they value the activities or products and expect to be successful. Students who are learning to play an instrument may already recognise the value of being able to play but might benefit from support in understanding the value of practice and the relation between practice and success.

**Attribution theory** provides useful insights for instrumental and singing teachers, suggesting that motivation to participate in an activity can depend on whether we regard success or failure as within our control. Where students view reasons for failure as being out of their control (an unfamiliar piano or an unfriendly examiner), they are less likely to continue with an activity. Where they recognise that they can have an impact on success and understand the relation between practice, ability and success, they are more likely to invest positively in their playing.

The age and ability of the individual will potentially affect the type of motivation most likely to succeed in encouraging them to practise. Younger and beginner students may respond to **extrinsic forms of motivation**, where the teacher or parent encourages specific behaviour by rewarding it with praise, certificates, stickers or treats. As the student develops and becomes more independent, they ideally begin to regard the act of playing and practising as rewarding and enjoy and recognise the benefits of regular practice without being persuaded or rewarded. This form of **intrinsic motivation** depends on the task being viewed as meaningful and worthwhile for the individual.

It is also important to consider what motivates students as learners, especially in relation to progress and success in instrumental music. Some students may be motivated by the need for *achievement* (or the need to avoid failure) and will work best when given targets such as exams, competitions and public performances. Other students may not respond positively to challenges of this kind and are more likely to succeed in manageable situations with frequent praise and encouragement.

Whatever the motivation, age or stage of development, a student will respond more positively when the level of challenge is in line with the skills of the individual. If the level of material and approach is too easy, they might become bored and if it is too difficult, they may be frustrated. It is the responsibility of the teacher to pitch the approach and set challenges at an appropriate level or the student may lose motivation and stop playing altogether.

# Teaching beginners

Support and encouragement are crucial for the beginner learner. Involving parents and carers to help develop regular practice habits can impact greatly on the experience and progress of the student. As the teacher, your role is to establish the foundations of instrumental playing, including safe technique, in an accessible and positive way.

> **Example: a first lesson with a beginner piano student**
>
> The main objective is to ensure that the student has an enjoyable musical experience with plenty of actual playing.
>
> *1. Start with a conversation about aims*
> *Why do you want to play the piano?* – and establish whether the student has a piano or keyboard at home, and if it is a keyboard what type it is.
>
> *2. Keyboard games*
> The lesson continues with games at the keyboard in which the teacher introduces the range of sounds available on a piano and encourages the student to identify notes. *This is middle C – see what it looks like? Can you find another C? Can you find an F? Can you play another F that will sound much lower than this one?* The teacher uses prompts from the earliest stages and encourages good hand position and posture.
>
> *3. Explore basic rhythms*
> The teacher introduces a basic rhythmic pattern and encourages the student to explore this in different places across the keyboard, playing by ear. This is followed by some call-and-response patterns on different notes.
>
> *4. Finger numbers*
> Introduce finger numbers and then the teacher asks the student to play specific notes with specific finger numbers. Note: if you are committed to introducing notation in the first session, it should be linked practically rather than as a separate entity. Perhaps consider only using rhythmic values to begin with and provide the student with exercises where basic patterns can be played on any notes and perhaps used to create their own tunes.
>
> *5. Develop listening skills*
> To encourage aural skills from the beginning, the teacher provides the rhythmic pattern from *Twinkle, twinkle* and encourages the student to work out the tune. The teacher then plays a basic accompaniment.
>
> *6. Set clear goals*
> At the end of the lesson, the teacher sets clear goals. Both the student and teacher keep notes and the teacher communicates with the parent either verbally or in writing.

As the student progresses, lessons will feature games and exercises to help develop listening skills and improve confidence at the keyboard along with elementary notation using either an established beginner course or material selected for the learning style of the student. Very simple duets are excellent for this stage as they provide scaffolding for the beginner player, encourage the student to maintain pulse and help build confidence.

**Top tips for working with beginners:**
- Support the student with praise and encouragement.
- Include a range of musical activities in each lesson.
- Ask regular questions to ensure the student is understanding fully.
- Involve parents and carers in the process, stressing the need to be supportive rather than critical at this stage.
- Involve the student in the choice of repertoire with a focus on fun, familiar and relevant material.
- Encourage the student to be creative and expressive from the outset.
- Keep a record of activities in each lesson and encourage the use of a practice diary.
- Agree specific practice goals in each session.

## Teaching intermediate learners

Perhaps the most difficult stage in instrumental teaching and learning is the period between the initial challenge of mastering basic skills and more advanced, independent playing. The intermediate learner needs to develop strategies for independent practice as they acquire more skill and their motivation becomes less extrinsic and more intrinsic. Students may still respond to rewards during this stage and the teacher should maintain regular communication with parents around practice and progress, but it is important that students understand the intrinsic benefits of practice as part of their development as independent learners.

During this stage you might involve the student in problem-solving activities and encourage them to take responsibility gradually for their learning, identifying strengths and weaknesses and developing a range of practice strategies. Lessons can therefore involve less scaffolding. The student may be more involved in identifying short and long-term goals along with specific repertoire choices.

Teachers might also encourage the student to join choirs, orchestras and ensembles to enhance their learning and benefit from the social experience of music making at this level. This can enhance motivation if the student identifies possible role models, group interests and goals.

Students can be motivated by exams and performances during the intermediate stage of learning but it is important to avoid simply progressing through the grades. Where students have acquired a degree of competency, instrumental lessons provide an opportunity to explore a range of musical styles and techniques in a rounded approach that can help to lay the foundations for success at a more advanced level.

### Example: planning an intermediate lesson

#### 1. *Start with a question*
*So what did you think worked well in your practice this week? Did you find anything especially tricky?* Use this initial conversation to set the tone and inform how you proceed with the warm-up.

#### 2. *Warm up*
*How can we make that sound stronger? How can we increase your breath control there? How does that feel? Where is that sound coming from? What should the bow hold look like? Show me how to stand/hold/breathe for this exercise?* Recognise what is working well and help the student to build problem-solving skills by working through solutions together.

#### 3. *New repertoire*
Perhaps start by playing or singing specific patterns, phrases or intervals as an exercise, using call and response. Build on these patterns and encourage the student to identify strategies for practising the piece. *Talk me through this passage. How could you practise it? How can we tackle this tricky area? What fingering would you use here?*

#### 4. *Existing repertoire*
Always give the student the opportunity to play through a piece or section of a piece they can perform with confidence. Perhaps accompany them. Provide feedback, recognising what is working well and ask how they feel about it. *How did that sound? How did it feel? How could you make it sound more dramatic, romantic, sad, grand, like a dance?* Agree strategies for development.

> **5.** *End of the lesson*
> Agree realistic goals for progress. *What do you think you could do this week with this piece?* Perhaps suggest some listening activities. Both make notes on specific issues covered during the lesson and your agreed goals for practice.

**Top tips for working with intermediate learners:**
- Maintain a fun and engaging approach to learning.
- Include a range of activities in each lesson.
- Don't assume that students want to take every/any grade exam.
- Agree short and long-term goals.
- Encourage the student to develop independent practice habits and to use a practice diary.
- Maintain contact with parents.
- Involve the student in problem solving.
- Explore a range of musical styles and genres.
- Involve the student in the choice of repertoire.
- Encourage the student to listen to a range of styles and genres.
- Keep a record of activities in each lesson.
- Encourage involvement in appropriate groups and ensembles.

## Teaching advanced learners

More advanced instrumental study requires commitment to regular, focussed practice and an awareness of long- and short-term aims, and the necessary strategies to achieve them. Advanced instrumental students may still need to be encouraged and supported in their practice habits but the way in which they practise is determined by understanding, established and reinforced by the teacher.

Advanced students are often motivated by performance goals such as concerts, exams, assessments or auditions. They should be able to identify technical challenges and have an understanding of specific tools and strategies to address them, as well as consideration of style and interpretation. The advanced instrumentalist or singer is more likely to engage positively if they feel they have contributed to the process, including choosing repertoire, improvising and devising their own material in an approach that supports and nurtures their creativity.

At this stage, your role as a teacher is to support this process by consistently reinforcing technical skills and problem-solving strategies and helping the student to set achievable short-term sub-goals for each practice session. Students at this stage can benefit from a broader range of ensemble opportunities in schools or music centres, and these activities can greatly enhance the experience of music making, providing an additional motivation to practise and progress.

### Example: planning an advanced lesson

Working with more advanced students should involve a significant level of input from the student. The student can also determine the focus of individual lessons where appropriate.

#### 1. *Warm up*
The student and teacher agree on a range of exercises to develop, consolidate and reinforce aspects of technique, ideally relating to the repertoire being studied in the lesson. Perhaps include call-and-response work using more complex patterns, style of articulation or technical exercises. Allow the student to demonstrate or lead rather than always following.

#### 2. *Repertoire work*
Having agreed short- and long-term goals with the student, the aim of the lesson is to work towards these goals by targeting specific passages or sections. When approaching new repertoire, start with some analysis of the style and genre and perhaps some exercises crafted from sections of the piece. Work through aspects of technique and, together, agree strategies for practice. Encourage the student to listen widely to the relevant style.

#### 3. *End of lesson*
Agree goals including practice strategies, and both student and teacher make notes on these. You may choose to agree a listening list.

**Top tips for working with advanced learners:**
- Agree long-term goals such as exams or performances.
- Involve the student in establishing short-term sub-goals.
- Encourage the student to identify their own strengths and weaknesses.
- Include a range of musical activities in each lesson.
- Involve the student in the choice of repertoire.
- Encourage the student to listen to a range of styles and genres.
- Encourage alternative modes of practice such as analysis and improvisation.
- Keep a record of activities in each lesson and encourage the use of a practice diary or notebook.
- Encourage involvement in group and ensemble activities.

# Group teaching

The challenge for instrumental teachers working with groups of students is to develop strategies that address the needs of each individual in the group whilst maintaining discipline and providing a meaningful and enjoyable musical experience for all involved. While the teacher is generally supported in classroom management by school staff, the approach to any group work requires considerable planning and preparation. Specific attention to the teaching space, resources and teaching strategies can help to ensure that activities cater for all students. If you take the time to develop a range of basic elements and extension activities around core exercises and pieces of repertoire, this can help to ensure that all participants benefit from the experience, whatever their ability. Children are used to group learning and will learn from both you and each other in these lessons. As musicians, we know all about the fun involved in making music with others – your goal is to share this with your students.

**Top tips for successful group lessons:**
- Plan a range of activities and be prepared to adapt them.
- Plan the teaching room so that each player has space for their instrument.
- Devise rhythmic patterns and harmonies to make sure that all players are engaged throughout.
- Ensure that all participants can join in at their level by modifying the material.
- Use call-and-response activities.
- Break down pieces into chunks and share these out to encourage concentration and develop aural skills, including pulse.

# What is good teaching?

> - Ask questions and encourage the participants to solve problems together, helping (scaffolding) each other if possible.
> - Have fun!

## Are exams a good idea and what are the alternatives?

Exams can provide a useful focus for some students, offering recognisable goals and motivating them to practise and progress. Many parents can regard exam success as the main purpose of study and this can influence students' perceptions. It is important to note, however, that exams are not for everyone and a more rounded approach that accommodates the interests and abilities of the individual student is recommended. For some students, exams can represent an unnecessary stress and impair both enjoyment and potential progress. Students may have no interest in formal activities including exams but simply want to play an instrument or sing, improvise or compose in the style they enjoy. As teachers, we need to adapt to each individual student, agreeing goals that match their interests and abilities and help to develop their creative potential, perhaps performing informal assessments or dropping in for occasional exams rather than working slavishly through every grade.

> **Top tips for successful teaching:**
> - *Be prepared*
> - Be positive and proactive
> - *Be prepared*
> - Always consider the student first
> - *Be prepared*
> - Try to have fun
> - *Be prepared*
> - Remember – every lesson counts
> - *Be prepared!*

**Recommended reading:**

Baker, D., & Green, L. (2013), 'Ear playing and aural development in the instrumental lesson: results from a 'case control' experiment', *Research studies in music education*, 35(2), 141–159.

Green, L. (2014), *Hear, listen, play! How to free your students' aural, improvisation and performance abilities*, Oxford: Oxford University Press.

Green, L. (2012), 'Musical 'learning styles' and 'learning strategies' in the instrumental lesson: Some emergent findings from a pilot study', *Psychology of music*, 40 (1), 42–65.

Green, L. (2008), *Music, informal learning and the school: a new classroom pedagogy*, Aldershot: Ashgate Publishers.

Green, L. (2002), *How popular musicians learn*, London: Routledge.

Hallam, S. (1998), *Instrumental teaching: a practical guide to better teaching and learning*, Oxford: Heinemann.

Harris, P. (2006), *Improve your teaching!: An essential handbook for instrumental and singing teachers*, London: Faber Music.

Harris, P. (2014), *Simultaneous learning: the definitive guide*, London: Faber Music.

Harris, P. (2015), *The virtuoso teacher: the inspirational guide for instrumental and singing teachers*, London: Faber Music.

Priest, P. (1989), 'Playing by ear: its nature and application to instrumental learning', *British Journal of Music Education*, 6(2), 173–191.

Varvarigou, M. & Green, L. (2014), The ear playing project, *Psychology of music*, 43(5), 705–722. earplaying.ioe.ac.uk

# 5
# Keeping safe

## Safeguarding

As a teacher you have a duty of care towards all of the students you are in contact with to ensure they are able to learn in a safe environment. If you have any concerns about a particular student or if a student shares confidential information, you need to know what appropriate action is required. You also need an awareness of what is considered appropriate and acceptable behaviour as a teacher, so your professional reputation is protected and you mitigate the chance of any allegations being made against you.

As an instrumental or singing teacher you are in a unique position – yours may be the only adult relationship your student has outside of the family unit. If you teach on a one-to-one basis, students might build a level of trust in you that leads to them sharing information that they wouldn't want to share with another teacher. Music is an emotive subject for many students and may bring up personal issues that could lead to a disclosure about a sensitive subject. You might also develop concerns about an individual student over a period of time, even as they move to different schools; you may notice changes in their demeanour or behaviour that other teachers do not.

Safeguarding involves learning when a judgement call needs to be made about a situation and when your concerns need to be passed on to an appropriate person, whether that is the parents or guardians, the school or another organisation who can advise on the best course of action. It is therefore important that you are always completely up to date with current practices and procedures regarding safeguarding so you know what your responsibilities are, both legal and moral, to your students.

During your teaching career you will probably have to teach in a variety of settings that could put you in a vulnerable position, such as in a student's home or in rooms that are not necessarily suitable for teaching. Often the work involves teaching students on a one-to-one basis. This chapter will advise how to minimise potential risks for you and suggest actions you can take to ensure that your behaviour is professional and not open to misinterpretation. We will also cover legislation that relates to this area for teachers, what constitutes child abuse, its signs and symptoms, the action required when concerns are raised and what your responsibilities are when working with children and young people.

Child protection can be a difficult and emotional subject for a teacher so it is important to take time to understand how these issues may affect you and your own teaching.

*How legislation affects us*

There are a number of pieces of legislation that cover safeguarding issues, and it is a subject that is under constant review. As a teacher it is strongly advised that you are aware of the current guidance and recommended good practice. Each time there is a serious child protection case there will an investigation and any subsequent recommendations may be written into law to avoid the situation being repeated and other children suffering similar outcomes. The laws and guidelines provide the legislative and regulatory framework for those working in the formal education sector.

**Keeping Children Safe in Education (KCSIE)**
The Department for Education produces guidance, updated each academic year, that educational institutions in England and Wales, including all schools, should adhere to. It can be found on the **gov.uk** website. In Scotland similar guidance can be found at **scotland.gov.uk** and in Northern Ireland at **northernireland.gov.uk**.

# Responsibility

Anyone under the age of 18 is considered to be a child in the educational system. Even though the statutory legal age for sexual consent is 16 in the UK, for anyone still in education the age that a consensual relationship is allowed is 18. It is considered an exploitation of a teacher's position of trust if they begin a relationship with a student whilst they are still within the education system. If the student is over the age of 18 then this is not illegal, but having a relationship with any student could be a breach of the teacher's contractual obligations even if the relationship is mutually consensual. Many institutions will prohibit relationships between students and teachers, whatever the age of the student. The advice here will always be **do not develop intimate personal relationships with your students**.

**KCSIE says**

'Safeguarding and promoting the welfare of children is everyone's responsibility. Everyone who comes into contact with children and their families and carers has a role to play in safeguarding children. In order to fulfil this responsibility, all professionals should make their approach child-centred. This means they should consider, at all times, what is in the best interest of the child.'

A **vulnerable adult** is anyone over the age of 18 who may need community services due to a mental or physical disability, who has incapacity due to age or illness or who is unable to take care of themselves or to protect themselves against significant harm or exploitation. Vulnerable adults are protected by legislation. You may well teach in situations where there are vulnerable adults so it is important that you know the relevant guidance and legislation for this work. Professional good practice as a musician engaged in any educational setting is usually transferable between working with vulnerable adults and children.

*What is the school's safeguarding responsibility?*
Schools have an important role in safeguarding their students. Each institution will have their own policies in place and a designated Child Protection Officer to whom all concerns and disclosures need to be reported. It is your responsibility to be aware of the safeguarding policy of each institution in which you work, and who is the designated person for safeguarding issues to be reported to.

*What is your safeguarding responsibility?*
You will need to ensure your teaching environment is as risk free as possible and that students are able to learn in a safe and secure environment. Acknowledge if your student might need extra help or if they could be at risk, taking appropriate action if required. You are not expected to be an expert in this field but you need to have enough knowledge and understanding to notice any concerns about your students and to know what to do about them.

*Safeguarding or child protection?*
**Safeguarding** applies to all children and is linked to promoting welfare, health and well-being to protect children from maltreatment and prevent any impairment of mental and physical health and development.

**Child protection** is an action taken to protect those children who are suffering or likely to suffer significant harm, abuse or neglect. Responsibility for child protection is spread across government agencies and institutions as well as individuals.

# Abuse and its effects on child development

As a teacher it is important to understand the impact and effect of child abuse on how a child develops.

The environment in which a child grows up – the family, the home, the neighbourhood, the school – plays a big role in how a child develops. During the early years, a child learns mainly through their interactions with their environment and with other people, therefore the stability of this period is crucial. This is how children begin to learn to solve problems, socialise, adopt good habits and develop the necessary motor skills and strength to function properly. If you have a student who seems at a different stage of development to their peers, it may be for a myriad of reasons, but it could indicate that there are issues that need addressing.

**Areas of child development include:**
- Physical – size, strength, motor control and coordination.
- Intellectual – thinking, learning and problem-solving abilities.
- Emotional and behavioural development – age-appropriate responses to events, recognising their own and others' emotions and being able to express feelings.
- Social – the skill to successfully interact with others.
- Moral – developing a conscience, differentiating right from wrong, understanding the impact of actions and words.

A *positive upbringing* will aim to preserve the innocence of the child by nurturing and protecting them whilst also investing time, energy and love into their lives. Children will thrive whatever their socio-economic status is if they have the support of a loving family and a stable and safe environment.

*Negative influences* on a child's upbringing include being in a household where there is a high risk of domestic abuse, substance abuse and mental ill health. The term 'toxic trio' is used to describe the combination of all three. Families who are identified as having these multiple and complex needs by relevant authorities require appropriate care and support to ensure that children are not experiencing unduly the negative effects of growing up with such problems.

There are also children who are considered more vulnerable because of their situation and these include **looked-after children** who are placed with foster parents or in a residential home, school or secure unit, and **asylum and refugee children** who have had to leave their home country where they were born or grew up.

As a teacher it is important that you are aware of the background of your students or any issues that could be detrimental to their development so you are able to know when concerns may need to be raised.

# Child abuse

Child abuse is the maltreatment of a child by inflicting harm or failing to act to prevent harm. Abuse can happen within a family setting or within an institution; perpetrators can be either adults or children. It can, and does, happen to children from any background, culture, class, faith or ethnicity.

As an educator it is your responsibility and duty to pass on any disclosures, allegations or concerns you might have to a designated person. Doing nothing if you have concerns can have high-risk outcomes, as it may be your report that helps to trigger an investigation that protects a child from being abused. It is not your role to be an investigator in child protection cases but only to report facts to the appropriate person in your setting.

All institutions should have a safeguarding policy and a dedicated Child Protection lead with the responsibility to receive safeguarding concerns and investigate appropriately. If you work privately from home, in your students' homes or in studios then it is recommended that you develop your own Safeguarding Policy to ensure a professional approach to your teaching practice and to protect yourself as well as your students.

*Forms of child abuse*
Having knowledge about the different forms of child abuse can help you identify what is happening if you feel there is an issue with one of your students.

Physical abuse is when someone hurts or harms a child on purpose. This includes:
– Hitting with hands or objects
– Slapping and punching
– Kicking
– Shaking
– Throwing
– Poisoning
– Burning and scalding
– Biting and scratching
– Drowning

Bumps and bruises don't always mean a child is being physically abused – all children have accidents, trips and falls. There isn't one sign or symptom to look out for but if a child regularly has injuries and there seems to be a pattern to the injuries, or the explanations as to what happened don't match then maybe concerns need to be raised.

Keeping safe

The effects of physical abuse can have long-lasting effects on children including anxiety and behavioural issues. Children who have been physically abused may develop eating disorders or drug and alcohol problems and will often have mental health issues that can include depression and suicidal tendencies.

> **Case study – physical abuse**
>
> Lucy had taught her student Sancha, aged 14, for a number of years and she had always been very happy and enthusiastic in her lessons. Over a period of time Lucy noticed that Sancha always wore long-sleeved jumpers even when it was very warm and didn't ever want to take the jumper off although it was obvious she was too hot in the lesson. Lucy noticed one day that Sancha had bruising down her arms when the sleeve of her jumper was pushed up. Some of the bruises looked recent but some of them looked older and resembled finger marks. Sancha noticed Lucy looking at her arms and immediately pulled down the sleeves of her jumper, mumbling about being clumsy. Sancha looked very distressed at this point and asked if she could leave the lesson. Lucy asked her if she was okay, to which Sancha replied 'Yes, of course', and went. Lucy was extremely concerned about her student so went to ask at the office if she could speak to the Deputy Head, who was the safeguarding lead at the school. The Deputy Head spoke to Lucy and said that she was right to report her concerns as the school had already noticed a change in Sancha's behaviour and were worried about her situation at home. They hadn't seen the bruising on her arms that could indicate some form of physical abuse that was happening.
>
> The school investigated the concerns and involved the Local Authority. Sancha's parents had separated, and she was living with her uncle who had been using physical force to keep her in the house; Sancha wanted to leave to go back to her mum.

**Neglect** is the ongoing failure to meet a child's basic needs, including food, cleanliness, clothing, shelter, supervision and appropriate health care. It is the most common form of child abuse; it could arise because parents or carers are in need of support or it could be systematic and deliberate. Neglect can put a child in danger and can also have a long-term effect on their physical and mental well-being.

Signs of child neglect:
- Poor appearance and hygiene issues.
- Being hungry and not having money or food at school.
- Not having warm clothes or a coat in winter.
- Wearing dirty clothes.

There might also be health and developmental problems. The child may be left unsupervised at home or taking on the role of carer for other family members.

Having one of these signs does not mean that a child is being neglected but if you notice multiple signs that are ongoing, it might indicate that there is a problem. The effects of neglect can be both short term (for example, the child experimenting with drugs and alcohol, running away from home and getting into dangerous relationships) and long term, as research shows that neglect can have an effect on brain development leading to mental health problems in later life.

### Case study – neglect

Leo, aged 9, had been learning drums with his teacher Tom for two terms. Leo seemed to be very small and underdeveloped for his age but was bright and able and very motivated to learn. Tom began to have concerns for his student when Leo started coming to lessons looking more and more unkempt, with dirty clothes that seemed too small for him. He also seemed to be constantly hungry and would eye any food that was around enviously. Tom once saw Leo picking up a discarded chocolate bar from the floor and at this point decided that he needed to raise his concerns with the school. He spoke to Leo's class teacher, who said that it was best if he spoke to the Headteacher as she was the safeguarding lead. Tom went to speak to the Headteacher who wrote down all his concerns and said she would investigate. It turned out that Leo's mum was struggling to look after Leo and his siblings as she had not been very well. The school was able to liaise with social services to provide the support needed until Leo's mum was better. The Headteacher thanked Tom for raising his concerns with the school as, although they aimed to be vigilant in their approach, Leo was in a class of 35 students and it was difficult sometimes to notice everything that was going on with each student.

When a child is **sexually abused** they are forced or tricked into sexual activities that they might not understand or know are wrong. They might be afraid to tell someone or are told they cannot tell anyone. They may feel it is their fault that it has happened or is happening. It is important to recognise that sexual abuse is never the child's fault and children need reassurance so that they know this to be true. Knowing the signs of sexual abuse can help give a voice to children.

There are two types of sexual abuse – contact and non-contact – and abuse can happen both in-person or online.

Signs of sexual abuse:
– Physical signs can include pains and soreness in the child's genital or anal areas or unexplained bruises, although sometimes these signs will be difficult to notice.
– Emotional and behavioural signs such as using sexual language or behaviour that is not age appropriate.
– Being frightened of spending time alone with someone or a group of people.
– Changes in behaviour that cannot be easily explained.
– Secrecy about who they are communicating with online or on their mobile phone.

Any child is at risk of being sexually abused, boys as well as girls, and for most the perpetrator is someone they know. This could be a family member, a friend or someone who has targeted them, such as a teacher or coach. Online abuse could be someone the child knows or someone who builds a relationship with them so abuse can happen. Some children are at more risk of abuse, such as those with disabilities, those who are isolated or those neglected by parents or carers, and it is important to provide these groups with the necessary safeguards.

The impact of sexual abuse can last a lifetime. Survivors may live with anxiety and depression, eating disorders, post-traumatic stress, self-harm, feelings of shame and guilt, drug and alcohol problems and difficulty in forming relationships.

### Case study – sexual abuse

Ali, aged 15, had been involved in the band project at the music centre for a couple of years and had good relations with all the other students there. When the term started again after the summer holiday, Sue noticed a big change in Ali's behaviour and appearance, as she now had new designer clothes each week as well as items of jewellery that she said were gifts. Sue noticed that Ali was picked up after band practice each week by an older man in a car and started having concerns about whom she was associating with. One week, Ali didn't turn up at the music centre but her mother appeared at the end of the practice looking for her. Sue told her mum that Ali wasn't there and saw that she was looking very concerned about her daughter. She told Sue that Ali was out every night. She didn't know where she was and who she was associating with. She also said that she and her daughter argued all the time now and communication had broken down. Sue told Ali's mum about the man she had seen picking up her daughter each week and that he seemed to be buying her expensive gifts. Sue encouraged Ali's mum to contact her daughter's school to help her talk to her daughter about who she was meeting and whether the concerns they both had were valid.

**Emotional or psychological abuse** describes the continual emotional mistreatment of a child. The signs of this form of abuse can be hard to spot, and it often (although not always) occurs at the same time as other forms of abuse that will, of course, affect a child emotionally. Parents or carers may not even acknowledge that their behaviour is inflicting emotional damage on the child.

There are many variations of emotional abuse:
– Deliberately trying to scare, humiliate, isolate or ignore the child.
– Constantly criticising the child.
– Blaming and scapegoating.
– Pushing a child too hard.
– Persistently ignoring the child.

As children grow up, their emotions change and it may be difficult to tell if they are being emotionally abused. There may be no obvious physical signs until the child reaches a crisis point, but the effects can be both behavioural and emotional and may lead to long-term mental health issues.

Signs of emotional abuse may include:
– Being unconfident or lacking in self-assurance.
– Struggling to control emotions.
– Acting in a way that is inappropriate for their age.
– Finding it difficult to make or maintain relationships.
– Unexplained changes in behaviour, such as not caring about the consequences of their actions.
– Trying to make people dislike them.
– Being unable to feel, express or control their emotions.

Any child from any background can be at risk of emotional abuse, although the risk is potentially higher when a family unit is having a challenging time and parents and carers might find it difficult to provide a safe and loving home for their children.

### Case study – emotional or psychological abuse

George, age 11, had started trumpet lessons the previous year and had made good progress initially with his teacher, Mario. Mario started having concerns about George when he began forgetting his trumpet for his lesson and making excuses why he couldn't practise at home. George seemed distracted and very anxious and didn't want Mario to contact his parents about missing his lessons. Mario asked George if there was anything wrong and he became tearful and said that he was being bullied when he brought his trumpet into school. Some boys in

> another year had taken his trumpet case off him and threatened to damage it; he had hidden it in a cupboard at school and didn't take it home with him. George asked Mario not to say anything as he didn't want to get into more trouble with the older boys. Mario knew that the school had an anti-bullying policy and said that this behaviour was not acceptable and George should not be intimidated into giving up playing the trumpet. George seemed relieved that the situation was going to be dealt with by his teacher and the school in the proper fashion.

There are a number of other forms of child abuse to make yourself aware of as a teacher, and these can be found on the NSPCC website: **nspcc.org.uk**.

## How to respond if a student confides in you

As a teacher, your student may want to share information with you about something that has happened to them. You have a duty of care to your students to ensure that you respond appropriately in the situation and know who to pass the information on to if needed.

**Do:**

- Be welcoming, even if it is awkward or difficult for you. It may have taken a great deal of courage for the student to approach you.
- Find a quiet place where you can have a private conversation without interruptions.
- Stay calm and listen carefully. Stay as neutral in your responses as possible.
- Allow the student to go at their own pace.
- Ask questions for clarification only.
- Communicate with them in an age appropriate way.
- Make notes, either at the time or as soon as possible afterwards. Note any names, dates, times.
- Be reassuring. Explain what you are going to do to help and what will happen next.

**Don't:**

- Don't display negative emotions such as shock, surprise, anger, distaste or dismay; it is okay to say that you are sorry this has happened to them.
- Don't make assumptions or prejudge; do not make comments about the situation or the abuser.
- You are not the investigator, so avoid asking leading questions.
- Don't promise confidentiality. If a student wants to talk to you but only if you promise not to tell anyone else then you cannot agree to this. It is your legal responsibility to pass on any concerns shared with you. If this means the child refuses to share any more information with you, then make a report to your safeguarding lead.

> **Case study**
>
> Chris, who worked for a music service, had taught Melissa (age 15) the guitar for a number of years and they enjoyed a good professional relationship. Melissa began to share with Chris in lessons that she was being bullied and had started self-harming, although she suggested that the situation had recently improved. Chris gave Melissa his mobile phone number and said to text him if she needed anyone to talk to. Melissa started texting Chris as a friend and he responded, trying to reassure her and offer advice. This exchange of messages went on for a while until Melissa's dad asked one day who she was texting. Melissa said that it was her guitar teacher; her dad was not at all happy. He contacted the music service to report what was happening and in the following investigation it transpired that Chris had known that Melissa was being bullied and had been self-harming, but had not passed this information on appropriately.
>
> Chris was given a final warning regarding his actions and Melissa was allocated to another teacher.
>
> *What did Chris do wrong?*
> - Gave his mobile number to a student to exchange messages that were not about the music lessons.
> - Befriended the student and took the relationship beyond that of teacher and student.
> - Failed to report that his student shared information about being bullied and self-harming.
>
> *What should he have done?*
> - Explained that he couldn't offer any advice or guidance as it wasn't his area of expertise.
> - Reported what Melissa had told him to the appropriate person, and informed her that he was doing so to ensure she would be supported.

## Reporting child abuse and the child protection system

The processes for reporting concerns are generally the same in all four countries of the UK, but it is worth making yourself familiar with the specific legislation of the country in which you are working. You should also familiarise yourself with the policies and reporting procedures for each organisation or institution in which you work.

**Step 1 Concerns are reported to the designated Child Protection Officer (CPO)**
If a student has shared sensitive information with you, regardless whether it is your student or not, then you need to report it to the designated Child Protection Officer (CPO) where you are working. Find out who the relevant person is and do not just report to anyone or ask them to pass the information on to the correct person. It is your duty of care to ensure that any concerns are reported appropriately. If you have not received a direct disclosure but have suspicions that a student is struggling for whatever reason then report it, as your concerns may add to the bigger picture.

If you are not teaching in an institution then you can report your concerns to the student's school, the Local Authority or the NSPCC.

**Step 2 The CPO will decide on the next course of action.** You may or may not be informed of what that is. If you feel that the situation has not been dealt with appropriately then you can raise your concerns again or escalate them to a higher level.

**Step 3 The CPO may refer the case to the Local Authority (LA) or the police.**
In extreme cases, if there is a risk to the life of the child or a risk of serious harm, then there will be an immediate strategy discussion involving children's social care, the police, healthcare professionals and other organisations to plan emergency action. This can be undertaken by the LA, social workers, the police or the NSPCC and may involve applying to the court for an Emergency Protection Order (EPO). If the risk is seen to be urgent and imminent the police can remove a child without an EPO.

**Step 4 The Local Authority's Children's Social Care board (CSC) will decide if further investigation is needed**, if the concern is not an immediate threat to the child. They will assess a child's needs and the parent's capacity to respond to them, and whether they are likely to suffer significant harm.

# Good practice for instrumental and singing teachers

Instrumental and singing teachers can be particularly vulnerable to false or malicious allegations against them because of the nature of the work. It is therefore really important that teachers behave as professionally as possible at all times to minimise the possibility of their behaviour being misinterpreted by their students.

Many allegations arise because the teacher has been naïve or may have not thought how their actions could be misinterpreted. Occasionally there will be a completely unfounded allegation made by a student, yet these still have to be investigated by the appropriate authorities and can be very traumatic for all involved.

Set boundaries and protocols within your own teaching and relationships with your students. It is a good idea to reflect on this and develop your own policies and strategies before you start teaching.

**Top tips for protecting yourself as a teacher**
- Keep a written record of all lessons. Note if something unusual happens that concerns you about the student's behaviour that you can refer to afterwards if needed.
- Always maintain professional standards when interacting with your students – how you dress, what information you share with them and what your expectations are regarding their behaviour in the lesson.
- Make yourself aware of all policies and procedures where you work regarding what is expected of you.
- Communicate with parents regarding your students' lessons and progress and make sure parents are copied in to any communication with your students. Keep all communication professional and open.
- Be visible – work in a room with a window if possible and let the student have a clear exit route. If you teach at home, or in your student's home, then have another adult present in the house if possible. Avoid teaching in your students' bedrooms or other rooms where you are isolated.
- Do a **risk assessment** on your teaching rooms if you feel that your own safety or that of your students is compromised. Report any concerns about room issues to the school or institution. A risk assessment determines possible mishaps, and their likelihood and consequences, as well as the tolerance for such events. Information on how to compile and use a risk assessment can be found on the Health and Safety Executive website.
- Avoid touching your students; explore creative ways of teaching that can be equally or even more effective for the student. This may feel time consuming initially but proper explanations and modelling of good technique and posture are worth the investment in the long term.

- Be mindful about your activity on social media and make sure that your professional life and your personal life are separated. Don't connect with students on your personal accounts and if you do use social media for work then keep all postings as professional as possible.
- Have a policy about how you communicate with your students that is acceptable to all, bearing in mind that some schools disallow any direct communication.
- Do not offer or give lifts in your car to a student. If you do not have business cover on your vehicle's insurance policy you may not be covered, and it also puts you in a very vulnerable position for any actions to be misinterpreted if you are alone with the student in the vehicle. If you have to give a lift to a student (if they are stranded, for example), make sure it is with the express permission of their parent/guardian and do not let it become standard practice.

## Allegations against teachers

In the event of an allegation, the teacher will be informed by the school or institution, or by the Local Authority or the police, depending on the nature of the allegation. Often there will be no details as to what the allegation is until the investigation has taken place and then the teacher will be asked to attend a meeting. The teacher may be suspended during this time in what is called a 'neutral act', depending on the seriousness of the allegation, and the teacher will continue to be paid if they are employed.

The school or institution will decide whether to carry out the initial investigation themselves, to pass it on to the Local Authority Designated Officer (LADO) or to report the incident to the police. Although it is good practice to investigate in a timely manner, it can be a long and drawn out process, especially if the police are involved. It is important that, as a teacher who is subject to an allegation against you, you have the right advice and guidance from the onset. Being a member of a trade union can be very helpful, as a specialist official will be able to advise you on your rights, and will attend, advise and advocate for you in meetings.

> ### Case study
>
> Aisling, a singing teacher, had started teaching in an all-girls' school. She was contacted one day after teaching by the Head to say that a complaint had been made against her. Aisling was devastated and asked what the complaint was. The Head said that they couldn't tell her at this juncture but she would be called into a meeting as soon as possible. Aisling contacted her trade union who said they would accompany her to the meeting. The following week, Aisling attended a meeting at the school with her trade union official, the Head and the Safeguarding Lead. The Head asked Aisling if she knew the allegations against her, and Aisling said no. She was told that two of Aisling's students alleged she had made them feel uncomfortable in the lessons because she had touched them to help with their breathing; if they had problems with rhythm, Aisling would tap the beat out on their arm. Aisling said she did do these things in the lesson, but only to help the students' progress, as that is how her own teacher had taught her. Aisling's trade union official asked the school if they had shared their safeguarding policies with Aisling and whether she had been asked to participate in any Child Protection training offered by the school.
>
> The school admitted that they hadn't shared any policies and procedures with Aisling and that no training had been offered. As she had only just started working at the school, they realised how important it was that all teachers knew what constituted acceptable behaviour with their students. The Head decided that she would explain the situation to the students and their parents and that Aisling needed to undertake Safeguarding training and to be aware of the specific policies of the school.
>
> Aisling was able to return to the school the following week and continue working with her singing students. After doing lots of research and talking with other teachers she realised that there were many ways of teaching breathing and rhythm that didn't involve touching the student. In considering this, Aisling actually thought that she had improved as a teacher as she was more thorough in her approach.

## Disclosure and Barring Service (DBS)

The DBS is an executive non-departmental public body sponsored by the Home Office. It provides checks on individuals in England, Wales, the Channel Islands and the Isle of Man and also maintains the adults' and children's lists of individuals who are barred from engaging in regulated activity.

The DBS perform background checks on an individual in order to ascertain whether they have criminal convictions, prosecutions or are barred from working with children or young people. This information will appear on the DBS certificate to help employers make safer recruitment decisions.

Teaching in most schools and institutions is considered a regulatory activity. It is a legal requirement that an individual has a current DBS check in order to carry out that work. There is also a service that individuals can apply for which allows the individual to keep their DBS certificates up-to-date and allows employers to check its status. You must apply for this service and register within 28 days of having the original certificate processed.

For more information visit **gov.uk**.

The process is run in Scotland by **Disclosure Scotland** and information can be found at **mygov.scot**. In Northern Ireland, **Access NI** is responsible for checks; information can be found at **nidirect.gov.uk**

## Safeguarding and child protection training

It is really important that you are up to date with the latest guidance and best practice in this area, therefore it is recommended that you participate in any training that is offered to you by the institutions or organisations that you work for. There is also a bespoke online course, Child Protection in Education (Music) that was developed by the Musicians' Union in partnership with Educare specifically for musicians who are working as teachers. The purpose of the course is to raise awareness of abuse, neglect and other harms, to help you recognise early signs that might indicate a problem and guide you on how to take appropriate action. The course is suitable for anyone who works with children in a music setting. It is a five-module course delivering five hours of Continual Professional Development. Details can be found at **educare.co.uk**.

For more information about reporting concerns about children visit **nspcc.og.uk**.

Free and confidential advice for children is available at **childline.org.uk**.

# 6

# Health and well-being for musicians

Health and well-being is an increasingly important part of musicians' training and the field of Performance Arts Medicine, covering the health issues of creative practitioners, is becoming a significant area for research. Unfortunately it is far too common for musicians to suffer playing-related injuries as well as develop hearing issues and have challenges to their mental health, affecting the individual in both the short and long term. The good news is that much of this can be avoided if care and consideration is taken whilst the student is still learning by raising awareness of these issues and sharing best practice guidelines.

As an educator, it is vital that you are aware of the importance of the health and well-being of your students at every level, as small changes in practice can produce significant gains for all musicians. The earlier good habits are formed, the more effective they will be in the long term.

Health and well-being can be thought about under four main headings: musculoskeletal health, vocal health, hearing health and mental health.

## Musculoskeletal health

*Why this matters*
Musicians learn a great deal about music, how their own instrument works and how to care for it. However, most are taught very little about their own body: how it works and how to care for it in relation to playing an instrument. Our bodies are such an integral part of producing music that they deserve the same attention and care we give to our instruments.

*Enhance your playing: keep well – play better*
It is important to remember the following key points:
- Moving with freedom and minimal tension can provide an ease of playing. Musicians will then be able to play and sing for longer before fatigue sets in.
- The enjoyment of playing or singing is enhanced if you are physically comfortable.
- Caring for our bodies can contribute to maximising the long-term sustainability of a career or hobby.

By incorporating strategies to help care for the body into students' lessons it becomes an integral part of their education.

## Safeguarding musculoskeletal health

Playing-related musculoskeletal disorders can and do happen to any musician and can range in severity from inconvenient to career ending. There are some evidence-based risk factors for playing-related musculoskeletal disorders in young musicians and being aware of what these are can enable teachers and parents to help students play safely and comfortably.

**Five risk factors for playing-related musculoskeletal disorders in young musicians**

**1 A sudden increase in playing time**

*Why this presents a risk*

In any activity, whether it is sport, fitness, dance or playing an instrument, if your body's soft tissues (muscles, tendons, ligaments and nerves) are not adequately ready or 'conditioned' to do more, there is risk of overuse that can cause straining, pain and injury, and reduce the ability to play.

*How to reduce the risk*
- Increase the time spent playing the instrument gradually, not suddenly.
- Help students manage their preparations for significant events such as exams, auditions and competitions.
- Encourage the use of visualisation techniques or 'mental practice' as a means to practise more without playing more: imagine the act of playing 'off instrument' to focus on details, iron out errors and correct fingering.

**2 The introduction of repertoire with a different technical demand**

*Why this presents a risk*

The body risks injury if a new activity is introduced suddenly. For musicians, new repertoire can present significantly different physical demands on the body.

*How to reduce the risk*
- Consider the repertoire from a physical perspective as well as from a musical one to minimise the risk of strain or injury.
- Think about where within a practice session the new repertoire is tackled. It makes sense to warm up with familiar repertoire, exercises, scales or studies, and then introduce the new material once the fingers are warm and playing easily, but before fatigue sets in.
- Practice sessions should use familiar activities to cool down before finishing.

## 3 Posture or position

*Why this presents a risk*
Instruments often place us in positions and postures that are far from neutral, which means that muscles, tendons, ligaments, joints and nerves are often required to work in positions that are (ergonomically speaking) less than ideal. This can lead to the overuse or underuse of some muscles and biomechanical strain on other soft tissues.

Playing in a fixed position for a protracted period is likely to become uncomfortable because accumulating tension can spread to other muscles resulting in fatigue, pain and changes in posture. With many instruments, the fingers or forearms may be very busy but the rest of the body can become rather fixed.

*How to reduce the risk*
- Encourage your students to take regular breaks from their playing by putting the instrument down and getting completely out of playing position.
- The British Association of Performing Arts Medicine (BAPAM) suggests that an adult player should take a ten minute break after 50 minutes of playing and the younger the player, the more frequent the breaks need to be.
- Be aware of a neutral position or posture that has less strain on the body, and try whenever possible to maintain components of it while playing. Return to it when not playing.

## 4 Stress

*Why this presents a risk*
Stress can lead to muscle tension. The specific muscles affected will vary from person to person, but it is common for the shoulder girdle, neck, jaw, hands and forearms (fist clenching) to be sites of tension when stressed. Holding your breath is also a sign of stress.

**Muscular tension has various effects:**
- Fatigue.
- A change in posture, reducing freedom of movement (for example in a bowing arm).
- A change in sound for a singer, woodwind or brass player if there's tension in the muscles of the neck, shoulder girdle or jaw.
- A detrimental effect on a person's ability to concentrate or learn.

*How to reduce the risk*
While it is not possible to eliminate stress from life, be aware that at various points students may feel stressed, and be mindful of the impact that it may have on their playing and learning. Being aware as a teacher of what stress factors may be impacting on your students allows you to adjust your expectations accordingly.

**5 Periods of rapid growth**

*Why this presents a risk*
Some children have periods of extremely rapid growth, and it is during or immediately after these growth spurts that children are particularly vulnerable to musculoskeletal problems.

Typically, the long bones grow first and then the soft tissues catch up with the new skeletal shape. For some young people these changes can impact their progress, especially during or immediately after a growth spurt.

There are three key changes at this point:
- The child is less flexible, as the soft tissues are effectively stretched over a larger frame.
- The muscles seem weaker as they are moving longer, heavier limbs.
- The child can become slightly less coordinated as they adapt to their new shape.

*How to reduce the risk*
- Avoid additional risk factors when a child is having a period of rapid growth, for example do not ask a child to increase playing time or add new repertoire with a different technical demand.
- It is also not the ideal time, however tempting, to change to a larger or heavier instrument. Allow the child or adolescent become used to their new body before asking them to get used to a new instrument.

*Communicating the foundations of good musculoskeletal health and well-being for musicians*
There are some simple strategies from the fields of dance and sport that can help music students maintain good musculoskeletal health and experience more comfortable playing and singing. Include the following techniques regularly in lessons so students can use them in their practice sessions.

# Health and well-being for musicians

## Strategies for good musculoskeletal health

### Before playing

*Warm up before tuning up*
Athletes and dancers begin every training session or performance by warming up. A warm-up increases blood flow to the muscles and helps reduce the risk of strain. It is called 'warming up' because you actually feel warmer! Warming up can easily be incorporated as a fun activity during lessons: try jogging on the spot, repeatedly move from sitting to standing, or step up and down on a bottom step for a minute.

*Limber up the specific muscles that will be used*
Prepare the joints and soft tissues by gently moving the parts of the body used during playing. This helps to remove tension and increase the student's awareness of how their body is feeling.

### During playing

*Be mindful of posture or any accumulation of tension*
Reset and return to a neutral position. Be aware of any accumulating tension and let it go. Take regular breaks.

### After playing

*Give your body as much care as you would your instrument*
Stretch the muscles that have been working hard or have been in a fixed playing position: the back, the neck, the shoulders and arms. Stretching helps to relax tense muscles, or muscles that have been working hard, and so can hugely increase how comfortable you feel after playing.

Promoting the health and well-being of musicians can only enhance the joy of making music. Incorporating an awareness of musculoskeletal health in instrumental and singing lessons from the very first encounter and sharing best practice can help to ensure safe teaching. The majority of playing-related injuries are preventable and instrumental teachers can help to avoid these issues by considering the health and well-being of their students at every stage in the learning process.

## Vocal health

Singers unfortunately often develop issues with their voices. Getting into good habits as early as possible and especially while still studying can significantly reduce vocal health problems later on. As a vocal teacher, passing on the correct information and advice to your students is imperative to them developing these good habits and techniques.

Instrumental or singing teachers are also at risk of experiencing vocal problems related to projecting or overusing the voice in educational settings. Being aware of these issues can help you to protect your voice and prevent damage.

Always encourage students to warm up physically before they sing. In particular, encourage them to stretch and loosen their neck, shoulders and upper back. This should be repeated after singing to cool down. Ensure all aspects of their technique are secure and reinforce these throughout the teaching process. Poor technical habits may lead to tension and muscular strain.

Check the student's posture and the balance in their body throughout the lesson, whether standing or sitting, to check for signs of tension, especially around the neck and shoulders. Check the music stand is at the right height for the student or, if they are holding their music, make sure it is not too heavy or bulky.

Encourage students to plan their practice sessions to allow short breaks (every 20 minutes is recommended). Make sure they are aware that if something starts to hurt they should stop and address the issue.

Be aware of the physical limitations of the body and adjust repertoire accordingly. If a student has a cold or sore throat, encourage rest and hydration. Signpost students to information about the importance of a healthy lifestyle as diet, a lack of sleep, drinking alcohol and smoking can all affect their vocal health. Talk to your students about being a 'musical athlete', and explain that taking care of yourself whilst studying will help you stay 'fit to perform'. Advocate the benefits of exercise and keeping physically fit as improvements to stamina and overall health will have a positive impact on vocal health.

## Mental health

As an instrumental or singing teacher, you are often an extremely important part of your student's educational life and development. Your role as a teacher is to encourage students to look after their mental health and psychological well-being as much as their physical health and to signpost further advice and help if needed. Being open about mental health issues is much more acceptable than it used to be.

There is a lot of stress and pressure on young people and there has been a significant increase in the use of mental health services by students in recent times. Research by Help Musicians UK found that over 70% of respondents to their survey had experienced high levels of anxiety and/or panic attacks. (**Gross and Musgrave, 2016**, *Can music make you sick? Music and depression*). Nearly the same level of respondents reported experiencing depression, meaning that musicians are three times more likely to experience depression than the national average.

Having a career as a musician can be all-encompassing with your work, income, creative outlet and social life all intertwined. If something happens to disrupt this it can have a devastating effect on individuals whose identity is completely wrapped up in their job.

**Top tips to share with students to help keep mentally healthy:**
- Encourage a healthy lifestyle, promoting positive habits around diet, exercise/fitness, weight, sleep and highlighting the negative effects of smoking, alcohol and substance abuse.
- Promote the benefits of self-care, encouraging students to allow time to look after themselves and decompress.
- Share methods for reducing excessive levels of tension, panic and anxiety, such as breathing technique and mindfulness.
- Set achievable goals for your students and try to balance other pressures such as school work, exams and their interests so they are not overwhelmed at any time.
- Be a good role model by showing a healthy attitude to the work-life balance.
- Look out for signs of 'burn out', when an exhausted and stressed-out body says it has had enough.
- Talk about boundaries that help differentiate where one role stops and another one starts. This can help the student know what is their responsibility and what is in the remit of someone else and can allow them to let go of things they don't need to hold on to.
- Be aware of networks that support young musicians. Encourage students to invest in building networks on which they can call in challenging times.
- Encourage resilience so that the student is able to recover after adversity, and to thrive and grow.

## Performance anxiety

Many musicians experience performance anxiety or 'stage fright', a situational form of anxiety. It happens when the brain registers a threat and the body responds by either moving towards or away from the threat ('fight or flight' mode). This feeling of fear, accompanied by increased bodily tension, can affect a performer when they are practising on their own, rehearsing with others, before and/or during a performance – in fact any time a performer is in a situation, competitive or not, where there is a dread of being judged or critiqued and found to be lacking.

Even though performance anxiety can be normalised to some extent, for some musicians it can become debilitating and is often cited as being a cause of musicians giving up performing. As a teacher it is beneficial to address any issues with your students as they arise and to talk about practical techniques they can use to help alleviate the issue. These may include breathing and relaxation techniques as well as positive visualisation and practising the voluntary management of tension in order to manage it.

Performance anxiety can be turned around and become a 'healthy stress' that can contribute to optimal performance. Again, it is worth having these conversations with your students so that this normal response to performing doesn't become extreme or develop into a disorder: Music Performance Anxiety (MPA).

## Hearing issues

Musicians can listen to and play music for hours each day, every day that can lead to hearing damage over time. As well as protecting your own hearing when necessary, you should inform your students of the potential dangers of listening to loud music and promote the benefits of wearing ear protection when appropriate. Almost any instrument can harm your hearing if played loudly enough over a long period and many professional musicians develop noise-induced hearing loss or other hearing issues over their careers that can be devastating.

There are things that you can do as a teacher to protect your own hearing. The quality of ear protection available in the form of earplugs has advanced enormously for musicians, allowing them to hear all of the music but at a lower sound level. If students see you using plugs when teaching, performing and practising it becomes normalised behaviour for young musicians. There are also things you can do to alleviate the effect of loud noise, such as standing to the side of other players, as sound travels in a straight line, or angling speakers away when playing with amplification. Take regular breaks, especially when practising, to give your ears a rest.

Be aware of situations that may increase the risk of exposure to loud noises, such as being in small practice rooms, teaching large groups and/or loud instruments and also teaching using amplification. All of these may have a cumulative effect of increasing the risk to your hearing and that of your students.

**Noise-induced hearing loss (NIHL)** is permanent and is the most common cause of hearing loss; it affects professional musicians more that the general public. Musicians are also more likely to develop other auditory issues, such as tinnitus (incessant ringing in the ears). NIHL is completely preventable, which is why protecting our ears and hearing is so important.

For more information about hearing issues for musicians and bespoke ear protection look at #HearForMusicians and the Musicians' Hearing Health Scheme.
musicianshearinghealthscheme.co.uk
musicianshearingservices.co.uk

# Further support

There are a number of specialist organisations that deal with all aspects of health and well-being for musicians and music students. Some of them offer advice, guidance and resources; some have helplines and some offer financial support for medical treatment or for those in need of assistance.

**The British Association for Performing Arts Medicine (BAPAM)** is a specialist healthcare charity supporting individuals and organisations in the performing arts. It provides free clinical services, expert training, essential resources and clinical leadership, and is regulated by the Care Quality Commission.
bapam.org.uk

**Help Musicians UK** provides support and opportunities to empower musicians at all stages of their lives. It is an independent charity that aims to make a difference to the lives of musicians by offering a wide spectrum of support including health and welfare services, a mental health helpline and funding for the hearing health scheme.
helpmusicians.org.uk

**Music Support** specialises in supporting those working in any areas of the music industry who are suffering from mental health or emotional health issues or addictions. They operate a telephone helpline offering peer support from volunteers with experience of the music industry and mental health and addiction matters.
musicsupport.org

**The Royal Society of Musicians** is Britain's oldest music charity providing financial assistance, advice and guidance to those who are professionally active in the world of music but who are unable to work due to accident, illness or old age.
rsmgb.org

**The Performing Rights Society Members' Fund** provides support and advice to PRS members and their families who may be struggling financially, physically or emotionally and are in need of help.
prsmembersfund.com

**The Healthy Conservatoire Network** aims to support environments that promote and enhance the health and well-being of performing artists, enabling them to achieve their full potential and to build healthy and sustainable careers. The HCN undertakes research on issues related to the health of performing artists and the website has useful resources to help performers and institutions work towards healthier practices, policies and provision.
healthyconservatoires.org

**The Musicians' Union** has many resources related to the health and well-being of musicians, including the *Music industry therapists' and coaches' (MITC) guide to anxiety relief and self isolation* and the *Young freelancer's guide to mental health and the music industry,* as well as regularly running online workshops on meditation techniques for musicians and Feldenkrais movement classes. Details can be found on the website.
themu.org

# 7

# Equality, diversity and inclusion

All those working in education need to ensure all their students have equal opportunities to learn, as set out in the Equality Act of 2010. Schools are expected to monitor their own policies regarding equality of opportunity and inclusivity and, as a teacher, it is important for you to be up to date with the policies and procedures of each of the individual institutions in which you work. If working independently as an instrumental or singing teacher it is also important to have your own strategies and policies in place to ensure that all of your teaching is as accessible and inclusive as possible for all students, so you can accommodate the needs of any student that may come to you.

Music is often cited as a subject area where it is possible to promote diversity and inclusion through a wide range of musical materials and tools and, as having musical talent does not depend on the background of the individual, it is an area where many students can really find an outlet for their creativity.

## Understanding discrimination

The Equality Act of 2010 makes it unlawful to discriminate against people on the following grounds:
- **Age** or because they are part of a particular age group.
- **Disability**, if they have or have had a physical or mental impairment that has a substantial and long-term adverse effect on that person's ability to carry out day-to-day activities.
- **Gender reassignment**, because they are considering transitioning, in the process of transitioning or have transitioned. The term transgender is an umbrella term to describe people whose gender identity is different to the gender assigned to them at birth. Individuals do not need to have had treatment or surgery to be considered transgender or to be protected by the Act.
- **Marriage and civil partnerships**, including people living together. Single people or people engaged or intending to marry are not protected.
- **Pregnancy and maternity**, because they are pregnant, have given birth recently, are breastfeeding or on maternity leave.
- **Race**, colour, nationality (including citizenship), ethnic or national origins.

- **Religion or belief**, or lack of belief. A belief needs to affect your life choices or the way you live for it to be included in the definition.
- **Sex**, your gender or perceived gender.
- **Sexual orientation**.

Discrimination on these grounds, known as **protected characteristics**, is unlawful for all education providers in relation to prospective students, current students, and former students with whom there is a continuing relationship. There are, however, some exceptions within the education system, such as faith schools and single sex schools, and some students that are disabled or have Special Educational Needs (SEN/D) may go to schools that support students with additional needs.

The **Equality Act** explains that having due regard for advancing equality involves:
- Removing or minimising disadvantages suffered by people due to their protected characteristic.
- Taking steps to meet the needs of people from protected groups where these are different from the needs of other people.
- Encouraging people from protected groups to participate in public life or in other activities where their participation is low.

The Equality Act states that meeting different needs involves taking steps to take account of disabilities, and that compliance may involve treating some people more favourably than others. This is something to consider within your teaching. Treating all students equally may actually discriminate unfairly against those who may need more support or guidance, so look at ways to address this.

> Have you experienced discrimination yourself or have you witnessed it?
>
> If so, what were the circumstances and how was it handled? Reflect on the situation and how it affected you or the people involved at the time and afterwards and how it could have been handled differently.

## Understanding diversity, equality and inclusion in music education

The concept of **equality** encompasses acceptance and respect. It means understanding that each individual is unique and recognizing our individual differences. These can be to do with race, ethnicity, gender, sexual orientation, socio-economic status, age, physical abilities, religious beliefs, political beliefs or other ideologies. Equality is about the exploration of these differences in a safe, positive and nurturing environment. It is also about understanding each other and moving beyond simple tolerance to embracing and celebrating the rich dimensions of diversity contained within each individual.

**Inclusion** in education is a pairing of the philosophy and pedagogical practices that allows each student to feel respected, confident and safe so they can learn and develop to their full potential. It is a system of values and beliefs based on the best interest of the student that promotes social cohesion, belonging, active participation in learning, a complete educational experience and positive interaction with peers. In an **inclusive** education, teachers value diversity and nurture the well-being and quality of learning from each of their students. Diversity in education is the foundation for an inclusive society.

**Equality** in music education means that personal or social circumstances such as gender, ethnic origin or family background are not obstacles to students achieving their potential and that all students have the opportunity to reach a basic level of skill. In education, **equality** may signify treating one individual differently to another and in the context of music education it may mean offering a range of different music making opportunities to ensure all students have equal access.

# Definitions of discrimination

**Direct discrimination** occurs when a student is treated less favourably than another because of a protected characteristic. It can also occur when they are associated with another person who has a protected characteristic or because they are mistakenly seen as having a protected characteristic.

**Indirect discrimination** occurs when treating all students in the same way results in putting students with a protected characteristic at a disadvantage.

**Discrimination arising from disability** occurs when a disabled student is treated unfavourably because of something related to their impairment and such treatment cannot be justified. Institutions have a duty to make reasonable adjustments for disabled students and prospective students as well as providing auxiliary aids and services if needed.

### Examples of discrimination: case studies

*Disability*
A violin teacher is told that one of his new students has been diagnosed as autistic. The teacher immediately decides that they won't be able to cope with learning the violin and excludes them from the lesson, recommending they should take up an instrument that's easier learn.

*Sex*
A class music teacher in a single sex girls' school has designed a curriculum that does not include the study of any female composers. When asked to include some female composers the teacher says that there are none worth considering.

A female student asks to learn the double bass. The teacher decides that this instrument is too big for the student as she's a girl. The teacher suggests something more manageable, like a flute.

*Race and ethnicity*
A class of primary school pupils are taking part in a whole class violin lesson project. The pupils are primarily from a Bengali background. The instrumental teacher decides that using western classical music is not appropriate as the students wouldn't understand it.

A student of colour tells their music teacher that they want to pursue a career as an orchestral musician. Their teacher says that there are very few orchestras that have any musicians of colour and maybe they would find it easier to become a professional musician in another area of the music industry.

*Sexual orientation*
A music teacher is made aware a student is being bullied for being a lesbian. The teacher takes no action as he decides that it is just teasing, and thinks it will prepare her for adult life.

A student wants to discuss LGBT+ composers. The teacher tells them that belonging to the LGBT+ community is 'wrong' and that they only teach heterosexual composers.

*Transgender*
A music teacher makes a decision to prevent a student who is transgender from attending a residential music camp because there isn't any suitable accommodation or toilet facilities for them. They make no effort to try and accommodate the student on the course.

*Religion or belief*
A Muslim student asks to reschedule a lesson so he can observe his religious commitments. This request is denied and he is told that he is required to attend the lesson. Later that week, the same teacher allows a Christian student to reschedule their lessons because they are preparing for their communion.

## What would you do?

1. A girl wants to play in a rock band but her father, who is paying for lessons, is against the idea. He doesn't believe girls should play in bands. Can this situation be challenged?

**Response:** *discuss the father's reservations with both (if possible) and explore the benefits of the girl's participation in ensemble activities. Find out if there is a compromise that can be reached that will satisfy the father and allow the daughter to take part.*

2. A Muslim girl wants to play the trombone – is that a suitable instrument for her?

**Response:** *yes, she should be offered the same opportunities as all other students; her choice of instrument should only be based on whether she has an interest in it.*

3. A student with Asperger's Syndrome continually disrupts the group with their challenging behaviour. How does this situation need to be handled?

**Response:** *depending on the student's condition and assuming that they are able to interact constructively within the group, allowances for the condition would be made in the teacher's preparation. But disruptive behaviour needs to be addressed as it would with any other student.*

4. A student who is a refugee only wants to play the drum each week and won't let other students have their turn. What tactics can be used here?

Response: *it is important that everyone gets the opportunity to play all the different instruments on offer in the session and the student may discover that if they play something else, they may enjoy it equally or even more. It is also important that the student learns to share and consider the wants of their peer group. Maybe remove the drum one week or play musical chairs with the instruments, swapping them regularly between students as a game.*

## Overcoming barriers to musical learning

In order to understand how to overcome barriers it is helpful to look at the different styles of learning and recognize that some may be more suitable than others.

- **Auditory learners** benefit from verbal instructions. They learn by listening and need to hear points being made verbally before they can act on them.

    Make sure that auditory learners are able to hear instructions properly and consider using recordings for the student to help consolidate their learning. Encourage them to read assignments and directions out loud to help them understand concepts.

- **Visual learners** benefit from seeing. These students value visual images and written notes and instructions for their learning experience.

    Make sure visual learners are able to see instructions properly and encourage visualisation techniques. Help them write down key words, ideas and instructions and use drawings, pictures and colour-coding to aid the learning process.

- **Kinaesthetic learners** learn by touching, feeling or experiencing through their own body. They acquire information by physical practice and often struggle with having to listen or read instructions for too long.

    Include activities that involve touching, building and moving around to increase the learning process.

Music lessons can be easily adapted to include all these activities and as a teacher, it is useful to experiment with a combination of different learning styles to make your teaching more inclusive, enjoyable and effective.

There are other factors that may be considered barriers to musical learning or participation:
- **Social** – peer pressure to pick an instrument or musical genre.
- **Cultural** – family or religious pressure determining a student's instrument choice or musical genre.
- **Gender assumptions** – historic gender association with instruments and genre; assumption of physical capabilities.
- **Learning difficulties** – level of literacy, attention span, frustration, anger or other emotions.
- **Physical Impairment** – access to where the lessons are held; the student's ability to hold and interact with the instrument.

# Technology-assisted learning

Assistive music technology can help widen access for students with Special Educational Needs or those who are disabled (SEN/D). This is an area that is improving all the time and the possibilities for engagement for SEN/D students is now much greater with digital solutions available that address access issues.

# Adapted instruments

There is a wide range of adaptive instruments available that have been specifically designed to make learning as accessible as possible. Many instruments can be adapted to accommodate the needs of a particular player and these should be explored before certain instruments are discarded as unsuitable for the individual.

**Top tips for promoting equality and diversity in musical learning:**
Always aim for an inclusive learning environment and be aware of the range of opportunities to help students engage and develop skills, knowledge and understanding in music.
- If you are working in a school, engage with the class teachers to find out which students might need extra support in their music lessons. They might have SEN/D or have English as an additional language (EAL), or be recognised as being gifted and talented (G&T).
- Find out what prior experiences the student has with music education and don't make assumptions about their starting point.
- Make sure your lessons include a variety of activities to engage the student across a range of learning styles (visual, auditory and kinaesthetic).

- If you are working with more than one student, your lesson plan should include differentiation that is appropriate to the students and their needs.
- Lesson plans need to include opportunities for assessment so that you know what students' needs are and can plan differentiation accordingly.
- Plan repertoire carefully to include the familiar and introduce the unfamiliar to ensure there is a real variety of music. Be creative and open to embracing music styles that may be unfamiliar to you but students listen to and want to play.
- Talk less in the lesson, as this may be a challenge for students still learning English or who find verbal instructions difficult.
- Plan a variety of teaching styles in your lessons, including learning to play by ear as well as using notation. Use elements such as improvisation and composition as well as set pieces. Using different approaches will ensure you are connecting most effectively with the students.
- Consider how you can make sure the materials you use for teaching are diverse and reflect the community you are teaching if possible. If you are aware that the composer of the music has a protected characteristic this could become part of the lesson to reinforce that anyone from any background can make music and be creative.
- Use history months and days to introduce music created by composers from minority backgrounds.
- Be aware of making assumptions that create problems for some students, such as whether they can easily practise at home, pay for lessons/books/exams/instruments, play in ensembles after school or at weekends, and also whether they are able to travel or wear certain clothes for concerts.
- Avoid potential barriers for learning such as setting work that is difficult to achieve for some students.
- Think about how you can engage all students during the lesson and avoid asking the same student to answer questions or give demonstrations.
- If you work in an institution then you can 'audit' how inclusive your teaching work is by considering how many of your students are entitled to free school meals, how many have a SEN/D diagnosis, how many are of a black or minority ethnic heritage and how many have English as an additional language. Also consider the gender balance of your students.

Considering all these facts will help you reflect on what you need to address and change in order for your teaching to become truly inclusive, which will benefit you as a teacher as well as your students.

## Useful resources

**Creative Futures:** *Sounding out* creativefuturesuk.com

**Drake Music:** *22 tips for inclusion accessibility in music education, The inclusion paper, Short guide to accessible music, Understanding disability, We all make music* drakemusic.org

**Fawcett Society:** *Gender stereotypes in early childhood – a literature review* fawcettsociety.org.uk

**Girl Guiding:** *Supporting trans young members* girlguiding.org.uk

**Guide to buying adaptive musical instruments:** takeitaway.org.uk

**Heart n Soul:** heartnsoul.co.uk

**Midlands Arts Centre:** *Music with children and young people who have social, emotional and mental health difficulties* macbirmingham.co.uk

**MU:** *Public sector equality duty, protected characteristics* musiciansunion.org.uk

**Music Mark:** *A short guide to working inclusively through music* musicmark.org.uk

**National Deaf Children's Society:** *How to make music activities accessible for deaf children and young people* musicmark.org.uk

**NEU:** *Boys' things and girls' things? Equality toolkit, It's just everywhere – sexism in schools, Stereotypes stop you doing stuff, Supporting trans and gender questioning students, 10 tips to tackle disablist language-based bullying in school – a guide for staff* neu.org.uk

**Runnymede Trust:** *Black and ethnic minority young people and educational disadvantage* runnymedetrust.org

**Scope:** *The social model of disability* scope.org.uk

**Sound connections:** *Increasing musical diversity and inclusion in early childhood settings* sound-connections.org.uk

**Youth Music with Drake Music:** *Do, review, improve... A quality framework for use in music-making sessions working with disabled young people and in SEN/D settings* network.youthmusic.org.uk

**Youth Music:** *Guidance for music education hubs – an inclusive approach* musicmark.org.uk

**Youth Music's Quality Framework and Youth Music Network's AMIE Resources:** network.youthmusic.org.uk

# 8

# What next?

It is important to keep up to date with current developments in music education, both general and specific, to maintain and enhance your existing practice. This chapter will look at **Continuing Professional Development (CPD)** and what it means for instrumental and singing teachers. It will discuss various forms of training and explore the idea of reflective practice. As already discussed in the introductory chapters, instrumental teachers can begin teaching with no formal training, and individuals can be engaged to teach in a broad range of contexts. Training and staff development opportunities may be available to those working for music services or institutions, but freelance teachers will need to find these opportunities for themselves. Taking the time to invest in training or Continuing Professional Development can refresh your skills, enhance your teaching, improve job satisfaction and also help maintain a connection to professional networks, which are a source of support in what can otherwise be an isolated professional role.

## What is CPD?

CPD is not something that can be done to you, it is something which you do yourself, sometimes unknowingly. Instrumental and singing teachers are constantly reworking, developing and enhancing existing roles, techniques and understanding. In this way, training for instrumental and singing teachers involves life-long learning and this ongoing process of learning on the job can be greatly enhanced through additional CPD activities. In a busy and predominantly freelance working life it can be very difficult to prioritise the time and resources to identify and participate in CPD, but these can be valuable and productive opportunities that can help you to stay motivated and satisfied in your work.

The term 'Continuing Professional Development' can refer to specific INSET (in service training) provisions arranged by institutions and specialist providers, specialist teaching or instrumental courses, or staff development training activities. In each of these situations the focus is on the acquisition and development of skills, knowledge and experience whether in formal or informal settings. This might involve workshops, masterclasses, formal teacher training, general sessions relating to teaching strategies and keeping up to date with legislation, technologies or new approaches.

## Where to start?

The first and most important task is to identify areas for development. These might relate to specialist knowledge, general teacher education or engagement with the instrumental and singing teaching community. Consider whether your goals relate to further qualification or the development of skills and understanding in less formal settings. There are various ways in which individuals can engage in CPD, from workshops and masterclasses to peer mentoring and online forums, and it is worth considering what type of opportunity appeals on a social level. Start by deciding which is the most interesting and suitable for you at the moment but remember that your needs, aims and interests will potentially develop throughout your career and you should regularly re-assess what might be appropriate and useful CPD for you.

## Taking stock

Take a moment here to consider your professional learning so far. Note what you have learned (and how) and which experiences have been most influential in developing your understanding and practice as a teacher. These experiences might have been formal or informal, intentional or accidental. Think about the main influences that have shaped your development. We don't always recognise everyday activities as learning opportunities, but consider how you have acquired your existing range of professional skills and understanding.

Perhaps you have developed your approach in one of the following ways:
- Trying something new and adapting or applying existing knowledge.
- Learning from mistakes or successes.
- Finding solutions to a problem or challenge.
- Working with and observing others.
- Being mentored or mentoring others.
- Reading about new approaches.
- Participating in an online forum or special interest group.

Now consider what you would like to achieve in the next phase of your career. This could be in the coming year or in the next three to five years.

*How are you feeling about your working life now?*
*Is there anything you would like to change or improve?*
*What would you like to do more of?*
*What would you like to do less of?*

# What next?

*Do you feel under-confident or less successful in any aspects of your work?*
*Have you any particular strengths you would like to further develop?*

These are important questions that we may not ask ourselves too often because we are focussed on juggling a range of roles and maintaining a productive working portfolio. However, these are essential considerations that can help determine the most appropriate form of CPD to support the future direction of your career.

## Planning your CPD

If you are interested in developing your career and acquiring new skills and knowledge, then CPD training can provide inspiration and ideas along with valuable opportunities to meet with other practitioners and expand your existing networks. Taking an interest in the work of others can provide inspiration, and you may gain satisfaction from sharing your skills and experience within a community of practice.

For some, a formal programme of study can be the most appropriate option, but less structured routes such as finding a professional mentor may also be of interest, depending on individual circumstances.

The following sections outline some of the learning opportunities available to musicians working as instrumental and singing teachers. These are divided into four categories to represent the ways in which individuals can participate in CDP activities. Some of the suggestions are simple steps that will help embed professional learning in your working life or keep you motivated and inspired. Others could help you make a significant change in your career. Ideally, you should choose two or three of the suggested activities and plan to action these over the next couple of years.

## Formal learning opportunities

Formal learning is a form of education that is structured in terms of time, objectives and resources, and often involves a rigid curriculum, leading to qualifications. This form of learning is usually organised and delivered in training or education institutions, workplaces and online. In contrast, informal learning can occur outside traditional learning environments, through encounters in the workplace and daily life or in learning projects.

For instrumental and singing teachers, the range of formal learning opportunities currently includes **MA** and **PGCE** programmes in instrumental and vocal teaching. Many UK universities offer modules in instrumental and vocal teaching as part of their music programmes. Some universities and conservatoires offer **Undergraduate** and **Master's degree** programmes in Music Education along with specialist PGCE courses. These opportunities provide a valuable source of training, incorporating the various practical and theoretical aspects of teaching. They can help develop skills and understanding, improve employment options and enhance career progression.

Musicians working as teachers can also benefit from other types of formal training. You might consider a course in **Alexander Technique** or **Dalcroze** that could benefit both your teaching and your own professional practice. You may choose to complete an instrument-specific training course to advance your skills as a teacher and increase your range of qualifications. Whether you are new to teaching or looking for ways to develop your skills, formal training in specific approaches such as the **Colour Strings** or **Suzuki** methods can provide a clear rationale for musicians involved in teaching.

For those who are interested in extending their range of options in music education, various organisations offer training in ensemble direction (choral and orchestral), including the **Association of British Choral Directors (ABCD)** and **Sing For Pleasure**.

**Formal learning opportunities**
- Apprenticeships and internships
- Short courses and workshops
- Postgraduate teaching qualification
- Professional accreditation
- Training programmes

# Accreditation and qualifications

Accreditation can be gained through a programme of study such as a PGCE or through 'self-accreditation' routes where practitioners submit evidence of existing knowledge and experience as instrumental and singing teachers. Training organisations, including some Further Education and Higher Education institutions, can provide accredited programmes of study in music education and community music practices leading to certificate and diploma qualifications. Some have an academic or research focus while others combine skills-based practical learning with an understanding of theory and ideas. The process of gaining accreditation can itself provide a valuable opportunity to reflect on individual practice in light of key ideas and approaches to teaching and learning.

Music membership organisations also offer one-off workshops and training opportunities, and in some cases work with other training providers to help support members in pursuing specific CPD activities.

## Reflective practice

This describes the process of thinking and reflecting on what we do and is closely linked to the concept of learning from experience. As an approach to CPD, reflective practice involves a conscious effort to think about events, activities and outcomes, and develop insights into them.

### Developing and using reflective practice

For instrumental and singing teachers, there are various ways in which we can learn and develop our skills and understandings using reflective practice. On a basic level, if we approach our own practice with an open and inquisitive mind, remain open to new or unfamiliar ideas, read about and explore our specialist area and share experiences and thoughts with other practitioners, then we are involved in reflective practice. This approach can increase self-awareness and develop creative thinking. It can improve our understanding of others and stimulate a more active engagement in our work.

- *Learning journals*

Keep a learning journal, detailing insights or inspirations from your day-to-day teaching as well as ideas from training events or activities. These notes can prove valuable as a way to review your development and inform your progression as a professional.

- *Action research*

Action research prioritises the knowledge and experience of the practitioner. In this approach, the practitioner explores a specific issue by asking questions and gathering evidence that is analysed to generate a greater understanding. This can be shared with the wider community of practitioners. Action research is a good way to expand on existing knowledge and connect with others working in the same field.

- *Mentoring*

Mentoring commonly involves a relationship with another, more experienced practitioner who might be able to provide both general and specialized support relating to teaching and career development. An effective mentoring relationship will involve conversations, observations and suggestions to help you enhance your existing practice and develop as a professional. This form of learning is especially appealing for instrumental and singing teaching as it is an extension of the apprenticeship model of tuition. Those interested in this form of CPD might consider approaching a more experienced teacher and asking to observe lessons as a first step.

Peer mentoring works on the same principal as traditional mentoring but usually takes place between individual practitioners of similar experience. This form of relationship is usually voluntary and can provide valuable support in the workplace, though for those working as freelance musicians, time may be limited. Again, to establish this form of mentoring relationship, consider discussing a potential partnership with another teacher in the same area or school.

**Reflective practice suggestions**
- Start a learning journal
- Action research
- Try something new
- Write down the most and least effective thing you do each week
- Establish peer-to-peer mentoring
- Become a professional mentor
- Set up your own group project

# Sharing best practice

How can we establish a mentoring relationship with other teachers when, as peripatetic and private tutors, we have so little contact with other staff? If you work in a school or music centre and would like to link with other teachers, perhaps start by suggesting a joint event such as a student showcase or a staff concert for charity. This would present a good way to build relationships by working together on a project and sharing best practice. This form of collaboration could then develop into a shared interest group or a mentoring relationship. If you work privately and have little contact with other teachers in your area, perhaps consider reaching out and inviting other local teachers to join you in putting on a student concert. The first step may seem daunting but establishing links with other musicians could open doors to many more opportunities, including peer learning.

**What next?**

## Connecting to a community of practice

A community of practice (CoP) is a group of people who are connected by a common concern or interest, who come together to fulfil both individual and group goals, offer ideas and strategies and create new knowledge to advance professional practice. Instrumental and singing teachers, especially those working on a freelance basis, can suffer from feelings of isolation and have little opportunity to work with others as part of a team. Joining a community of practice such as a membership organisation, a network, an online community or even an informal group of colleagues can make a great difference to the professional experience and provides an excellent opportunity to share, learn and develop existing skills.

Who can you talk to about your work? Do support groups or specific organisations exist that could help you achieve your goals? Are you currently a member of any music organisations? There is much to gain both professionally and socially from joining a specialist organisation or society. As a first step, perhaps consider joining a society for instrumental or singing teachers. There are many to choose from, but a good place to start is one that is instrument specific, such as EPTA – European Piano Teachers' Association; EVTA – European Voice Teachers' Association, BVS – British Viola Society; WBA and EBA – World and European Brass Association. These are a great source of information and resources.

**Connecting to a community of practice**
- Attend a network event or conference.
- Engage with your local music education hub.
- Subscribe to a journal or e-news service.
- Join a network or membership organisation.
- Form your own community of interest.
- Read a case study online or create your own and share it!

## Social learning activities and initiatives

Social learning involves learning from other people though observing, asking questions or sharing knowledge. Observing the materials, resources and communication strategies used by other teachers, including the ways they approach technical problems, can be a valuable learning opportunity and a great way to reflect on your own practice. Similarly, having another teacher observe your teaching can help to highlight the strengths in your approach as well as areas where you might need further development.

While this notion may be intimidating for some, observations that take place in a relationship where the participants are mutually respectful and supportive can be a rewarding and productive experience. It is worth establishing the level of commitment in advance, being mindful to manage expectations of the time required for all involved.

> **Social learning activities**
> - Observe a lesson – discuss your approach and that of others.
> - Ask a peer to observe you and give feedback.
> - Go to a performance of someone else's students.
> - Take part in a webinar or online chat.
> - Talk with colleagues about what is going well and what is not.
> - Read relevant research.

Whichever form of CPD you find most attractive, the most important thing is to make the first step and start your journey. Whether you research and apply for a formal course, join a membership group, arrange to observe a colleague's teaching, seek out new reading and resources or simply start to reflect on your own practice in a more methodical way, every opportunity to develop your knowledge is valuable. These activities can help to ensure your role as an instrumental or singing teacher is successful and rewarding and will have a significant impact on your future career in this field.

### Suggested reading:
Hallam, S. & Gaunt, H, (2012), *Preparing for success: a practical guide for young musicians*, London: Institute of Education
Harris, P. (2006), *Improve your teaching!* London: Faber Music.
Harris, P. (2014), *Simultaneous learning: the definitive guide,* London: Faber Music.
Harris, P. (2015), *The virtuoso teacher*, London: Faber Music.
Williams, A. (2017), *The piano teacher's survival guide*, London: Faber Music.

### Useful websites:
*PGCE in music with specialist instrumental teaching:* **rncm.ac.uk**
*PGCE in secondary music with specialist instrument teaching:* **mmu.ac.uk**
alexanderteacher.co.uk
estastrings.org.uk
colourstrings.fi
britishsuzuki.org.uk
abcd.org.uk
dalcroze.org.uk/dalcroze-training
singforpleasure.org.uk

**Notes**

Notes

## Notes

# Notes

# Also available

**The Complete Practice Workbook** (Harris)
This indispensable resource supports every aspect of instrumental practice, including a diary, Simultaneous Learning practice map, and space for ideas, notes and music.

**Group Music Teaching in Practice** (Davies and Harris)
An invaluable resource for all music leaders and teachers involved in delivering group teaching programmes.

**Improve Your Teaching!** (Harris)
The must-have handbook for all instrumental and singing teachers. Packed with comprehensive advice and practical strategies, this is a modern and holistic approach to teaching music.

**Musicians' Union Practice Diary** (Harris)
A must-have practice diary that is based on Paul Harris's Simultaneous Learning approach. Featuring *Focus for the week*, *What we did in the lesson*, practice starter pages and holiday projects.

**The Piano Teacher's Survival Guide** (Williams)
Featuring many case studies, music examples and problem-solving clinics, this is a rich resource of basic principles, useful tools and thought-provoking ideas.

**Simultaneous Learning** (Harris)
In this definitive guide, Paul Harris outlines the complete philosophy of his ground-breaking teaching approach.

**Teaching Beginners** (Harris)
Distilled from years of personal experience and research, Paul Harris looks at the issues concerning teaching beginners, offering a series of principles, advice and strategies.

**The Virtuoso Teacher** (Harris)
This seminal book is an inspirational read for all music teachers, encouraging everyone to consider themselves in a new and uplifted light.

Available to buy online and from all good music retailers.
Visit **fabermusic.com**